The Diaper Bag Book for Toddlers

Authors

Robin Dodson and Jan Mades, M.A.

Editor: *Casey Null*

Editorial Project Manager: *Mara Ellen Guckian*

Editor-in-Chief: *Sharon Coan, M.S. Ed.*

Publishers: *Rachelle Cracchiolo, M.S. Ed.*
Mary Dupuy Smith, M.S. Ed.

Product Manager: *Phil Garcia*

Illustrators: *Alexandra Artigas, Kevin Barnes*
Kevin McCarthy, Kelly McMahon

Art Directors: *Lee Aucoin, Cjae Froshay*

Art Manager: *Kevin Barnes*

Imaging: *Rosa C. See, James Edward Grace*

Cover Design: *Neri Garcia*

Teacher Created Materials, Inc.
6421 Industry Way
Westminster, CA 92683
www.teachercreated.com

©2004 Teacher Created Materials, Inc.
Made in U.S.A.
ISBN #0-7439-3758-9

Table of Contents

Table of Contents (cont.)

Introduction

You are your child's first and most important teacher. Over the years, you will set the tone for your child's feelings of confidence and competence as he faces challenges. A child who has been provided a variety of activities, allowed to experience success, encouraged to try again after a setback, and loved regardless of his performance, is developing the attitudes about himself and learning that promote success in school.

Most of the activities in this book require little or no equipment or materials and can be done on the spur of the moment. Keeping up with a busy toddler doesn't leave much time for elaborate plans. It is in the unfolding of everyday life that your child does most of his learning. One of the most important things you can do is TALK to him. We think with words. When you increase his vocabulary by connecting his everyday experiences with the corresponding words, you are actually building the foundation for conceptual thought.

Young children learn best through exploration and imitation. The suggestions in this book will provide lots of opportunities for discovery, trial and error, and repetition. In the context of a supportive relationship, a child will feel secure enough to try new things, make mistakes, and persevere. Your child will respond to your encouragement and acknowledgement of his efforts with increasing confidence. You will be preparing your child not only for school but also for a bright, fulfilling future.

How to Use This Book

You can start anywhere you'd like. The activities are grouped according to where you might find yourself during a typical day. There is an age-group breakdown within each section which suggests the earliest age to introduce an activity. Feel free to try activities from the proceeding age group. Toddlers like doing things well. Simpler activities give them confidence and a sense of mastery. Working on the same developmental skill in a variety of ways helps broaden and deepen your toddler's understanding of that skill. Many of the activities list variations to adjust the difficulty. Allow your child to make mistakes, and expect a lot of repetition before a new accomplishment occurs.

Toddlers have short attention spans. Expect variations in their interest level and ability to focus. Keeping a toddler at an activity longer than he wants leads to frustration. Keep playtime fun by following your toddler's lead. Relax and enjoy your toddler. New learning occurs through repeated and varied exposure to a skill over time, combined with developmental maturity. You can't control the rate of development, but you can provide the exposure to a variety of activities that promote the building of key skills.

The greatest gift you can give your child is the support he needs to become the person he was meant to be, according to the inner timetable he is following. Have fun and know that the simple everyday activities you share will provide a strong foundation for the years to come.

The 18-24 Month Old

The young toddler begins to assert her separateness through the words *no*, *me*, and *mine*, and seemingly resistant behavior. This "stubbornness" comes from her growing sense of independence; she now has strong *wants* in addition to needs. It isn't always easy to tell what she's thinking.

A toddler can become very frustrated with her lack of language skills and inability to express herself clearly. Tantrums are very common. Conversely, an 18–24 month old may not separate from a parent easily. She struggles with feeling empowered by her growing independence ("Hey! I can walk away from you!") and frightened by it ("Hey! That means you could walk away from me!"). She still needs emotional support through cuddle time and reassurance even though she needs you less physically.

Young toddlers are always on the move. Their physical development takes precedence. Don't expect her to sit for long. Socially, a child this age plays best by herself, although she may like being around other children. She will treat them as objects without feelings, and may push or bite to get what she wants. Close supervision, short play dates, and open-ended play activites will help your toddler have successful social experiences.

The 24-30 Month Old

The middle toddler's increase in language skills helps decrease his frustration level. His vocabulary may "explode," increasing rapidly to over 900 words by the age of three. He is calmer, and delights in seeing his day unfold with sameness and order. It is comforting for him to be able to anticipate what happens next in the routine.

He becomes more confident in his motor skills. He is able to open doors and locks and climbs well. Middle toddlers want to participate in the world and show interest in helping with household tasks including vacuuming, emptying the dishwasher, and sweeping. He will want to play next to others, maybe do the same things they do, but probably won't directly interact just yet. This developmental stage is commonly known as *side-by-side play*. His thinking is still very concrete. He may take language literally and misunderstand phrases like "I'm going to eat you up" or "You're my little peanut."

The 30-36 Month Old

Rapid development creates an unstable time in the life of your older toddler. She will probably potty train. She will find a first friend. She will become more difficult and demanding, and say "NO" to just about everything. She can get very intense very quickly. This can be expressed with aggressive behaviors like kicking or biting. She will overestimate her independence and capabilities ("I don't need to hold your hand in the parking lot!"). She will be frustrated with the rules and limits placed upon her ("Sorry toddler, you can't drive the car.").

Older toddlers are pretty certain they know how to do everything, and now that they have more speech, they expect to get anything they request. It's tough being two-and-a-half. Your toddler may revert to thumb sucking, or stuttering, or stuttering as a way to relieve some tension. She will come to understand limits and boundaries and settle down as she nears three years of age. Don't take her development personally.

Areas of Development

Gross Motor Development

Gross motor development requires the coordination of movement of the body's large muscles—walking, running, jumping with two feet, throwing, and kicking. Bilateral movements require the limbs on the right side of the body to perform actions in opposition to the ones on the left side—alternating feet while climbing stairs, pedaling a tricycle, and swimming. When the right and left sides of the body are doing different movements, the brain has to coordinate information between the right and left hemispheres, stimulating the brain development necessary for higher-level skills like reading.

Fine Motor Development

Fine motor development refers to any movement that requires the coordination of the muscles in the wrists, hands, and fingers. These skills are required to pick up tiny objects, stack small blocks, zip or button clothing, string beads, open jars, and later hold and use a crayon or pencil properly.

Social-Emotional Development

Social-Emotional Development includes self-esteem, separating from parents, independence, playing with others, recognizing emotions, understanding limits, and gaining self-control. Toddlers gain physical independence from us (self-feeding, toileting) before emotional independence. Toddlers will learn about social skills and expressing emotions from observing and imitating the adults around them. Mastery of social-emotional skills is years away.

Areas of Development (cont.)

Cognitive Development

Early cognitive (thinking) skills include understanding simple cause-and-effect relationships, early symbolic thought, recognizing same and different, understanding spatial relationships, sorting objects into categories (animals, clothing, foods) and understanding simple concepts like color, size, and shape. Cognitive growth continues with sequencing, understanding patterns and the ability to compare and contrast. Most growth in this area occurs in the pre-school years. Toddler cognitive growth is interrelated with language development.

Language Development

A toddler has a large *receptive vocabulary*. A toddler understands many more words than she can say. Expressive skills progress from single words to phrases and sentences. Building vocabulary is paramount during the toddler years. At first, a toddler speaks mostly with nouns and a few verbs. Her concrete thinking skills understand objects and actions best. Introducing and repeating words for concepts like color, shape, size, and spatial relationships while a toddler experiences them help her connect the right word to the right concept. This in turn builds the brain's cognitive ability to think abstractly. Also important to language development is the auditory discrimination of sounds. This leads to distinguishing words, and then letter sounds.

Areas of Development (cont.)

Pre-math Skills: Toddlers need repeated exposure to concepts like quantity (*few, many, more* and *less*), size (*big* and *little*), length (*long* and *short*) and time (*now* and *later, yesterday* and *tomorrow*) before they are ready to understand these concepts in numerical form. Working with these concepts in a variety of ways is more important than learning to count at this age. Other early math skills include matching, sorting, sequencing, patterning, and 1-to-1 correspondence. Hands-on experiences with the concepts work in combination with the corresponding vocabulary words to help toddlers form the abstract thinking necessary for higher mathematical concepts.

Pre-literacy Skills: These skills include understanding that written words record our thoughts (grocery list, stories, letters to grandparents) and a that book tells the same story in the same sequence. Auditory discrimination skills allow for identifying sounds (clock ticking, doorbell, traffic), differentiating letter sounds, and rhyming. Visual skills needed include discrimination to tell letters apart, and visual tracking skills to follow left-to-right orientation. The most important things you can do to build pre-literacy skills and prepare your child for reading is to build vocabulary and READ aloud to her. Take advantage of your local library to supplement your child's personal collection.

Diaper Distractions

Toddlers can be squirmy and resistant at diaper changing time. It is one of the classic situations where she asserts her independence at the wrong place and time. Let her hold an object with which she's not normally allowed to play. She may lie still if she's got your watch, a wooden figurine, a small picture frame, or even a kitchen utensil to examine.

Try reciting some of her favorite finger plays to keep her hands busy and her mind focused.

This is also a good opportunity to use temporal (time concept) words. *Now* it's time to change your diaper; *after* that we will.... *then* we can....

Materials: household objects

Developing Skills

- understanding limits
- spatial/temporal concepts
- sequencing

Bathtub Crayons

These thick and sturdy crayons are just right for toddlers. Add one teaspoon of food coloring to one cup of laundry soap flakes (not detergent). Add water by the teaspoonful, stirring constantly, until the soap dissolves into a paste. Press the paste into ice cube trays. Let dry for a few days, until hard. The cube crayons are ready for your toddler to draw on the bathtub walls.

Materials: soap flakes, food coloring, ice cube trays

Developing Skills

- fine motor coordination
- creativity

The Dressing/Undressing Song

Sing to the tune of "My Darling Clementine."

Take your jammies off,
Take your jammies off,
Take your jammies off, just like this.
Pull your arms out, take your head out,
Slide the pants off, just like this.

Put your shirt on, put your shirt on,
Put your shirt on, just like this.
Put your head in, put your arm in,
Now the other arm, just like this.

Pull your pants on, pull your pants on,
Pull your pants on, just like this,
First your right leg, then your left leg,
Pull them up now, just like this.

Developing Skills

- sequencing
- social-emotional
- independence/self-help skills

Toddlers thrive on routines. They look forward to knowing what comes next. Sing "The Dressing/Undressing" song to help establish a pattern for dressing and undressing for your toddler. Established routines diminish the power struggles that will come with the next stage of independence.

Mealtime Mess

By now, your toddler will insist upon feeding herself, but her ability to connect cause and effect will most likely be demonstrated with the repetitive science experiment, "If I turn this bowl over, will the food fall out?" The best defense is to give her only small amounts of finger food. Skip the bowl altogether and place the food directly on her high chair tray. Look at this as an opportunity to increase her language ability as she asks for more. She can get practice dumping out with her toys.

Developing Skills

- fine motor coordination
- expressive language

High Chair Fix

Your toddler is working on her gross motor skills by climbing out of the high chair. A way to slow down this occurrence is to have her sit down and then right before you close the tray across the top, place a rolling pin or rolled towel under her legs right at the end of the seat of the chair. She should have plenty of room to sit comfortably but not have enough room to pull her legs out from under the tray to get to the standing position. This is just a stage and it, too, shall pass.

Materials: rolling pin or towel

Developing Skills

* understanding limits

Nap Choices

Balking at taking a nap can mean your toddler is testing her independence, or she is having separation issues. Young children need more sleep than adults. Try suggesting naps with options, "Do you want to rest on mommy's bed or your bed?" or "Do you want to rest with Huggy Bear or with your fuzzy crocodile?" There may be days when she just doesn't fall asleep. The rule has to be to stay in the room until rest time is over. Sometimes, just lying down with her to read a story helps and it doesn't hurt you to get a few winks, either. Keep nap time in the daily routine. This quiet time will develop into independent reading time or homework time as she grows.

Materials: none

Developing Skills

- social-emotional: independence or separation
- understanding limits

Books In Bed

Leave a few sturdy board books in the crib with your toddler. It gives her something to do when she wakes up in the morning. With something to do, she may not call for you immediately. Also, "reading" to herself builds her aptitude for independent play.

Materials: board books

Developing Skills

- pre-literacy: books tell a story
- social-emotional: independence

Egg Beater Bubbles

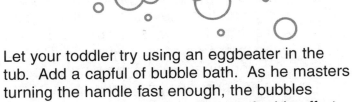

Let your toddler try using an eggbeater in the tub. Add a capful of bubble bath. As he masters turning the handle fast enough, the bubbles formed will give him reinforcement for his efforts.

Variation: Try a tabletop version with dish soap in a dishpan or in the sink.

Materials: hand-operated eggbeater, bubble bath

Developing Skills

- fine motor coordination
- sensory motor play

Water Toys

Small plastic spice jars, with all the parts of the lids, make some of the best water toys. The jars float if the lids are screwed on tightly. Unscrew the lids and leave just the shaker part of the lid on and the jars will sink slowly as the air bubbles out. It's great science fun to experiment with what floats and what sinks while taking a bath. Also, language development takes place as you use the following words: *rub, pat, dry, wet, screw, unscrew, turn, float, sink, take apart, put together, squeeze, spin, roll, push, pull, blow, open, close.*

Materials: empty plastic spice jars

Developing Skills

- vocabulary enrichment
- spatial-temporal concepts
- fine motor coordination

Dressing Distractions

When your toddler wants to do it himself but can't quite, try a substitution. Have him dress a doll while you dress him. Make sure there are simple clothes to put on dolly while you are busy with the difficult finishing touches of getting him dressed. Or, try dressing your toddler in front of the mirror. He can watch the transformation he goes through.

Materials: doll, simple doll clothes, mirror

Developing Skills

- social-emotional: self-awareness
- fine motor coordination
- understanding limits

Drinking from a Cup

Drinking from an open cup is a developmental skill. Your toddler needs to understand how to handle the cup, without spilling, by lifting it with a controlled motion and tipping it to his lips at just the right time. He has a lot to pay attention to and many adjustments to make throughout the process which makes for a wet learning process. A covered, no-spill cup doesn't offer any consequence for mishandling so learning is minimal. Save the covered cup for traveling. At regular mealtimes, when he is seated, offer his drink in a real cup. Start with water and fill the cup only half way.

Materials: small plastic cup

Developing Skills

- fine motor coordination
- social-emotional: self-help skills
- cause and effect

Family Placemats

Soon it will be time for your toddler to be moved from his high chair to a booster seat at the table where he will feel more like part of the family. Make a special placemat for meal times. First, take individual pictures of everyone in your family. Then mount each individual picture onto a seperate 8" x 11" (20 cm x 28 cm) piece of paper. Next draw an outline for the cup, plate, and silverware. This can be a matching activity, too. Cover each placemat with clear shelf paper to make them waterproof. Most toddlers are not able to sit through an entire meal and conversation, too! Help him down as soon as he is finished eating. His attention span will grow with every year and before you know it he will be sitting for the duration.

Materials: snapshots of each family member, paper, clear shelf paper

Developing Skills

- social-emotional: self-esteem
- cognitive: matching
- social-emotional: independence

Daily Reading

Books provide an interactive experience for your toddler and they can play a larger role now that he has more language skills. In addition to naming and pointing to objects in books, ask him to find something red, or tall, or wet in the picture. Be sure to reverse roles and let your toddler direct you. Build his thinking skills by asking him, "What comes next?" before turning the page. Ask him about character motivation with a simple, "Why did he do that?" or "Why does she want that?" It is interesting to see your toddlers limited ability to take another's point of view.

Materials: children's books

Developing Skills

- cognitive: abstract thinking
- pre-literacy: sequencing, predicting
- memory

Bedtime Foot Massage

If your two-year-old no longer sleeps in a crib, he will likely pop out of bed just because he can. Now that you can sit on his bed, try a foot massage to help him get relaxed and sleepy. Place a special lotion in his bedtime basket. As you rub his feet (not tickle them!) you can tell a bedtime story instead of reading one. This is a great way to share family history and give your toddler a sense of family identity. Perhaps you will add bedtime prayers or nighttime wishes to the ritual. It's a special ending of the day to remind him of your love. Remember, a routine helps him predict and accept what's coming next.

Materials: baby lotion

Developing Skills

- understanding limits
- social-emotional: self-esteem
- tactile stimulation

Writing on the Wall

Squirt a few blobs of shaving cream on the water's surface at bath time. Let your child have some squishy, gooey fun poking and playing. Next, squirt some foam on the tub wall. Smear it around and let your child draw with her fingertips. Let your child draw at will. You can "erase" by smearing a wet hand over the designs.

Variations: After plenty of free-form figures, introduce simple shapes like a circle or cross. Show your child how to trace her finger over the shape you made. Encourage her to try to make a shape, too. Play for as long as your child seems interested.

Materials: can of foamy shaving cream, tub of warm water

Developing Skills

- fine motor skills
- sensory motor exploration

Water Words

Children learn best through repeated experience and bath time is one of the best times to develop language. Purchase some different-textured (natural and artificial) sponges. Get enough so you can demonstrate the difference between rough and smooth, bumpy, flat, etc. Cut them to child size, including different thicknesses. Keep them all in one bucket. Be sure to use the following attributes to describe them: *soft, hard, rough, smooth, big, little, short, long, thick, thin, hot, cold, wet, dry, heavy, light, straight, curved.*

Variation: Ask her to, "Give me a rough sponge. Give me a thin sponge." Ask her to identify a sponge with her eyes closed.

Materials: various sponges

Developing Skills

- vocabulary enrichment: attributes
- fine motor coordination
- concepts: size, shape, opposites
- sensory descrimination

Swimming Skills

The bathtub is a great place to adjust to water before real swimming lessons start. Your toddler should feel comfortable with water poured on her face. Start with just a cupful poured gently on her shoulder while you talk playfully about the experience. Move on to include her cheek, side of head, back of head, and top of head. Teach her to fully inflate her cheeks and keep her lips closed. This seals off the nose from the inside. Call them "bubble cheeks" to help her remember. Teach her to blow bubbles with her mouth and later out her nose (like humming). She can also practice opening her eyes underwater. Put a small object in your palm and hold it underwater. Reveal it only when your toddler looks from underwater. There is no rush, so don't push her beyond her comfort level. Her confidence will increase when she is in control of the timetable.

Materials: none

Developing Skills

- water adjustment
- social-emotional: self-esteem

Balls and Nets

Put some plastic practice golf balls in the bathtub. Get both the kinds with holes and with solid surfaces. Some will sink and some will float. Now let your toddler fish them out with a little net. She can scoop them into a colander as you count them.

Variation: Set this up in your sensory table box

Materials: plastic golf balls, goldfish net, plastic colander

Developing Skills

- eye-hand coordination
- pre-math: exposure to counting

Nap Sacks

Some older twos may temporarily develop the habit of napping only every other day and then returning, eventually, to a short daily nap. Here is a suggestion for those days when sleep just doesn't seem to come. Make several different "nap sacks" and give your toddler a choice at naptime. She can pick one and it can only be played with on the bed during the rest period.

Sack 1: Large interlocking plastic blocks.

Sack 2: Old-fashioned tablet that she scratches on and then pulls up to erase, or a magnetic drawing pad.

Sack 3: Large snap-together beads (large enough to not be a choking hazard).

Sack 4: Very special books (lift the flaps, I Spy books, etc.).

Sack 5: Any kind of manipulative blocks.

Sack 6: Lacing cards

Sack 7: Magazines

Developing Skills

- social-emotional: independence
- understanding limits

Materials: 7 small sacks, bins, or pillowcases

Essentials for Bed

The older toddler has discovered the power of language and will use it in her battle to stay up past her bedtime. Don't let repeated requests become routine. Have everything ready before she asks. Instead of a million trips to the bathroom for a drink of water give her a special nighttime "sippy" cup so she can give herself a drink without getting up. Does she like to hear a certain bedtime music tape or have a favorite book in bed or her "snuggly"? Be sure it's all by her bedside. Remember to arrange the door or a night light just the way she likes it.

Materials: none

Developing Skills

- social-emotional: independence
- understanding limits

Bedtime: Mommy Is Reading

Settling in at the end of the day can be a difficult transition. A nightly ritual helps but there will still be those nights when your little one refuses to stay in bed. When that happens, assure her that she is not missing out on any fun by taking this time to have a relaxing end to your day as well. Bring your book to read just outside her door. Sit on the floor where she can see you but focus your attention on the book. Do not engage in conversation. Just say, "It's time for bed and I need to read."

Materials: grown-up reading materials

Developing Skills

- pre-literacy: modeling reading
- understanding limits

Why Household Chores?

Allowing your toddler to help with chores is one way to promote self-esteem and emotional growth. Only a few tasks can actually be accomplished at this age, but by working together you empower your toddler with the knowledge that he is an important member of the family. He feels appreciated and competent when you genuinely thank him for his contributions. Even though including him will take longer, it is easier than having him play by himself while you work. He wants to be near you and is interested in imitating what you do. This is an opportunity to establish helping behaviors before he realizes that this is work and not play. Don't save all your chores for nap time anymore.

Doing laundry, preparing meals, and cleaning are opportunities to spend quality time together. Each time you include your toddler, you can teach new vocabulary, demonstrate spatial relationships, introduce attributes like color, size, shape, and lay the foundation for science and math. Most importantly, you give your toddler a chance to master skills and take pride in his growing independence. Is this play? Is this work? Yes, but most importantly, it's learning!

Laundry Learning

Let your toddler help you gather all the things that need to be washed. As you strip the beds, make a pile of linens and let him jump in it. If you have steps in your house, practice jumping off a specially marked step (for instance, use masking tape to mark the **x** on the 2nd step) into the pile of dirty clothes. He will have gross motor practice as he works his arm muscles carrying clothes to the laundry area. Next comes the sorting into appropriate piles. Laundry sorting can be a vocabulary experience as you name the textures and colors. Play a quick round of basketball by tossing every piece of white clothing into one basket before filling the next one with the darks.

Materials: piles of dirty laundry

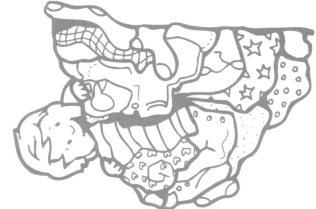

Developing Skills

- gross motor development
- vocabulary enrichment: attributes
- cognitive: sorting and matching

Laundry

Toddlers love to fetch things. They also like to feel helpful. Direct some of that physical energy with this laundry day suggestion. Let your toddler pull some of the clothes out of the dryer.

Caution: Make sure clothes and dryer are not hot.

Let him dump the basket of clothes out on the carpet or on a clean sheet. Dumping things out is another favorite activity! Sit with the empty basket a few feet away from the pile of clothes. Ask your child to bring you different items of clothing as you fold. Say, "Bring me a sock." "Find another sock." Fold the items as he brings them to you and place them in the basket.

Materials: clean, unfolded laundry; laundry basket

Developing Skills

- purposeful movement
- self-esteem
- sense of independence

Mealtime Clean Up

Your toddler can help with the after-mealtime clean up. Ask him to wipe his face. Of course you may need to do a bit of a touch–up. Have him carry his plate to you at the sink. He can also throw any trash in the garbage. Let him wipe his high chair tray. It doesn't matter if the job is done well at this stage. Just teaching him that he is a capable and contributing member of the family is enough and it sets a foundation for later responsibility. Remember to thank him for his help.

Materials: small face cloth and a kitchen sponge

Developing Skills

- social-emotional: self-esteem
- social-emotional: independence/self-help skills
- following directions

Scrubbing the Floors & Driving the Bus

It's time to wash the kitchen floor. Let your toddler help remove the chairs from the kitchen. He can push the chairs and you can arrange them in a line to create a bus (or airplane, or train). A plastic plate makes a good steering wheel. Your toddler can get some of his stuffed animals to go for a ride. If you give him a small amount of water and a sponge of his own, or a dusting cloth, he can help clean the "bus seats" before they are returned to the kitchen. He gets to play; you get to finish scrubbing the floor.

Materials: kitchen chairs, small sponge or dusting cloth

Developing Skills

- gross motor coordination
- cognitive skills: symbolic representation
- pretend play

Empty the Dishwasher or Dish Drainer

After the dishwasher has finished its cycle and the contents have cooled (or the items in the dish drainer have had time to air dry), remove the sharp knives and fragile items. Now your toddler can help unload the rest (move dish drainer to a table). Ask him to find a spoon and hand it to you. Now find another. He will have to look closely. Ask him to hand you the cups. Continue as long as he is interested.

Variation: Ask for specific items like the red cup or Mommy's cheese grater.

Materials: kitchen items

Developing Skills

- following directions
- cognitive: sorting
- receptive language

Organize the Toys

Help your toddler know where to put things away. If there are too many toys to fit on his shelves, consider storing some out of sight, in a closet. Too many choices overwhelm toddlers. Rotate the toys on a weekly basis. Cut the picture of a toy from the box in which it came. Tape the picture on the toy shelf where the toy belongs. If a toy has a lot of pieces, tape the picture on the side of a plastic storage bin that can hold them all. "A place for everything and everything in its place" helps your toddler organize his inner world as well.

Materials: plastic storage bins, tape, toy box pictures

Developing Skills

- cognitive: matching and sorting
- social-emotional: independence/ self-help skills

Dusting

Toddlers like to imitate adults and show interest in household tasks. They may ask to push the vacuum or use a broom. A dust cloth is small enough for a toddler to handle. Cut a few 6" (15 cm) squares of felt or flannel. A dark color shows the dust best. You can demonstrate with one cloth while your toddler imitates with the other. Low bookshelves are ideal. Your toddler will enjoy watching the dust appear on the cloth after she wipes a shelf. What a great excuse to let the furniture get really dusty before you clean it!

Materials: felt or flannel cloth

Developing Skills

- social-emotional: independence
- cause and effect
- fine motor coordination

Clean Windows

Developing Skills

- fine motor coordination
- cognitive: shapes
- pre-writing

A wax made for polishing glass can be rubbed on all shiny surfaces (appliances, glass). Apply the wax to a window and allow it to dry to a cloudy film. Give your toddler a small piece of soft cloth. Teach her to wrap her finger in the cloth so she can draw designs on the cloudy surface. Can she trace or copy simple shapes? You can leave the window decorated all day but when evening comes, use a soft cloth to buff the entire surface. You now have a clean window that resists finger smudges until it's time to do it all again. **Cautions:** Supervise your toddler as she draws. Teach her not to push too hard. If she must use a stepstool, stand close by. Glass wax can be toxic if ingested in large amounts, so never let your toddler apply the product herself and have her wash her hands when finished.

Materials: glass wax, soft cloth

Washing Walls/Cupboards

Toddlers love to imitate and perform real tasks alongside us. Some chores, however, are just too much for toddlers' attention spans and abilities. For those big jobs, you can set up a situation so your little one can join you, leave, and come back and help again.

Use a large blanket or sheet to turn your kitchen table or a couple of chairs into a tent stocked with some toys that have been put away for a while. Your toddler can choose between helping you or playing in her special space near you. This gives you time to finish a big cleaning job. Always equip her with a small bucket and kid-size sponge so she can wash the bottom cupboards or side of the fridge as many times as she wants.

Materials: large blanket or sheet, toys, small sponge, bucket

Developing Skills

- fine motor coordination
- cognitive: attributes
- vocabulary enrichment

Sharky, Sharky

Pretend that your vacuum is a shark that chases your toddler. Before starting the game, establish what places in your house will be safe zones or "boats." It's fun to take a cushion off a chair or couch and designate it as a "boat." This is a great activity to do when cabin fever strikes. Your toddler can run from boat to boat and even scream as she flees from the shark. Another great thing is that the ocean gets turned back into a floor when the vacuuming is finished, "boats" return to chairs and it becomes time to read a book to restore calm after all the excitement.

Materials: vacuum cleaner

Developing Skills

- cognitive: symbolic representation
- understanding limits
- pretend play

More Laundry Learning

Matching and sorting are perfect laundry activities. The challenge progresses from finding all the socks, to sorting the socks by color, to matching the identical pairs of small, white socks and Daddy's big blue socks. Other tasks with which your two-year-old can help are putting clothes in the washing machine, adding the soap, and transferring clothes to the dryer. These tasks provide an excellent vocabulary-enriching opportunity. Following are some words that can be demonstrated and experienced by the chore at hand:

open, close, empty, full, wet, dry, heavy, light, rough, smooth, light, dark, colors, easy, hard, wash, dry, pour, more, less, few, many, all, some, same, different, these, those, that one, this one.

Materials: clean laundry

Developing Skills

- fine motor coordination
- cognitive: attributes, mathematical groupings, matching, sorting
- vocabulary enrichment

Clean Up Time

Include your toddler in the daily clean-up routine. A messy room is one giant sorting activity! Your toddler won't know where to start. This song gives specific, concrete directions that are easier to understand than broad statements like "clean this up."

Developing Skills

- cognitive: sorting
- social-emotional: self-help skills
- directions

(Sing to the tune, "Row, Row, Row Your Boat.")

Clean, clean, clean your room,
Put it all away.
Books go on the bookshelf
'Til another day.

Additional verses: Change the third line to:

Clothes go in the hamper.
Blocks go in the block box.
Toys go in the basket.

Last verse:

Clean, clean, clean your room,
It's all put away.
Well done, give a cheer
Hurray, hurray, hurray!

Garden Help

A garden is a perfect place for science lessons. Start seeds in egg cartons to transplant in a child-only patch next to the adult garden. Observing the changes during the growing cycle are well worth the mess. The easiest task to teach is how to prepare the soil. Two-year-olds can hoe with the best of them. Add daily watering with a toy watering can. Teach her how to pull weeds once the plants are established and growing taller than the weeds. Because little fingers sometimes get eager and pull out the real plants, too, it's a good idea to have some extras growing in the adult garden to transplant. You will be surprised at how excited she will be to see her very own plants grow. **Variation:** Plant grass seed in a plastic cup to keep indoors. She can cut the grass with scissors. **Materials:** paper egg carton, garden seeds, child-size garden tools and watering can

Developing Skills

- fine and gross motor coordination
- cognitive: cause-and-effect sequence
- vocabulary enrichment

Washing Windows

It takes some skill to operate a spray bottle. It uses the same movements as cutting with scissors. Fill a small spray bottle with water. This looks like glass cleaner, but is non-toxic. Let your toddler clean the sliding glass door, the refrigerator, laminate cabinet doors, and the floor. Provide him with a cloth or paper towel to wipe and dry. He may want to repeat the activity right after he just cleaned something. It is the process and the movement that is attractive to toddlers, not the finished product.

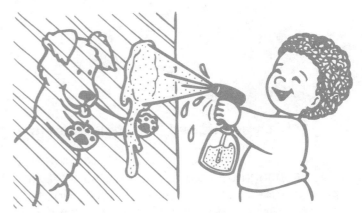

Developing Skills

- fine motor coordination
- social-emotional: independence

Materials: small trigger spray bottle, paper towel or cloth

Caution: Make certain your child does not have access to cleaning products in similar containers. Explain that you have made a special, safe spray bottle just for him (or her).

Clean Sweep

Buy a little dustpan and brush set (not a toy) for your toddler. Find the smallest one you can that will work well. Store it where your toddler can easily reach it. Now when you sweep the kitchen floor, he can brush up the piles you make. Show him how to dump the dirt in a wastebasket. Don't expect perfection. You will probably have to clean up after all his help. He will feel important when his contributions are appreciated.

Materials: small dust pan and brush

Developing Skills

- fine motor coordination
- social-emotional: independence
- social-emotional: self-esteem

Pour It On

Use a small pitcher to teach your toddler to pour. A creamer, measuring cup, or child's plastic pitcher works well. Fill it with just enough milk (or soy/rice milk) to pour on his bowl of morning cereal. Show him how to pour slowly by pouring the liquid on your bowl of cereal first. Refill the pitcher and let him pour the liquid in his bowl. He may use a dumping motion at first. With practice, he will be able to control his movements.

Variation: Let your toddler pour from a small pitcher into two cups. Use water, at first, to ease clean up. You will show him a vote of confidence when you let him pour the morning orange juice for the family.

Materials: a creamer, one-cup liquid measuring cup with handle, or small pitcher

Developing Skills

- social-emotional: self-esteem
- fine motor coordination
- social-emotional: independence/self-help skills

Refrigerator Snacks

Can your toddler open the refrigerator by himself? Rather than making it off limits, consider designating an area that he can use. Define the space with a little tray on one of the lower shelves. Put a few snack items on the tray that you wouldn't mind him having free access to. Suggestions include small containers of yogurt or cottage cheese, cut-up grapes or orange sections, a few crackers, and a covered cup of water or juice. Now your toddler can get himself a snack when he wants to. At first, he may be so enamored with the idea that he eats all of his snacks before lunch. Over time, the novelty will wear off and he will use it more in response to his actual hunger.

Materials: small tray

Developing Skills

- social-emotional: independence
- social-emotional: self-help skills
- social-emotional: self-control

Setting the Table

Your two-year-old is beginning to understand one-to-one relationships. He builds on this skill when he helps you set the table. It may take longer to get the task done, but the opportunities for learning are great and well worth the effort. Ask him to get a spoon for each person. He may first name one family member, then get one spoon, then put it on the table. He will repeat this one-to-one process for everybody. Help him stay on track. Make placemats from construction paper and outline the plate, cup, and utensils. This will help him to do the job independently. He knows he is finished when he has everything set on the paper mats.

Materials: construction paper, markers, clear shelf paper

Developing Skills

- social-emotional: independence
- pre-math: one-to-one correspondence
- fine motor coordination

Napkin Folding

This is a follow-up activity to setting the table. It improves fine motor ability but takes some real practice to do correctly. Give your child the napkins and have him lay one at each place. Then show him how to lift two corners of each napkin with just the thumb and index fingers and fold across to meet the opposite edge of the napkin. Press and crease the fold. Then place the napkin under the fork.

Materials: paper or cloth napkins

Developing Skills

- spatial relationships
- visual discrimination
- fine motor coordination

Mr. or Ms. Fix It

Our children love to copy us and do real things. A two-year-old is developing the eye-hand coordination it takes to use a hammer. He is not ready, however, to do the whole task by himself. The key is to have the right size hammer. It needs to be small enough to get his hands around and lightweight. Get some short nails with big heads. Drive a few nails about half way into some scrap wood. Next time you have a project, let him pound in the nails the rest of the way. He may use two hands at first.

Materials: scrap wood, a small hammer, nails

Developing Skills

- eye-hand coordination
- social-emotional: self-esteem
- fine motor coordination

Hide and Seek 1

Gather a few of your toddler's small toys (a stuffed animal, a little truck, a ball, a board book). Hide them around the living room with your child so she sees where they are hidden. Now, sit down and ask your toddler to "Bring me the truck," "Go find your book," etc., until all the hidden items have been retrieved. If she brings the wrong item cheerfully say, "You brought me the ball, now where is that truck?"

Variations: The difficulty level can be changed by making the items fully visible, partially visible, or completely hidden.

Materials: 3–4 small toys

Developing Skills

- receptive language
- memory
- purposeful movement

Grocery Bag Blocks

Let your toddler help you tear and crumple old newspapers. Stuff paper grocery bags about half full with the newspaper. Fold the top over and securely tape it shut to make "blocks." Make at least four or five blocks. Decorate them with crayon, marker, and/or stickers. These stack and topple safely, giving her opportunities to reach, bend, build, and kick.

Materials: paper grocery bags, old newspaper, wide tape, crayons or markers, stickers

Developing Skills

- fine motor coordination
- gross motor coordination

Stop and Go Music

Help your toddler learn to control her body with this game. Play any music you like. Randomly pause it. You can reinforce this with the verbal cue, "Stop." Leave the music stopped until she stands still. It is hard to stop on cue at first. Start the music again, and say, "Go." At first you will need to dance, too, in order to model how to stop and start when the music does. Next, see if she can stop and go with just the music for a cue.

Variation: Use a rhythm band instrument (see homemade ideas on the next page). Shake and stop it to the music.

Materials: radio or CD player

Developing Skills

- listening skills
- social-emotional: self-control
- gross motor coordination

Homemade Rhythm Band Instruments

- Drill or poke a hole through three juice can lids. Attach them together loosely with a chenille stick (pipe cleaner).
- String together several jingle bells on a chenille stick (pipe cleaner).
- Make a tambourine by putting dried beans inside two paper plates. Tape or staple around the edges of the plates to seal in the beans.
- Make different sounding shakers by putting dry rice, beans, sand, or noodles inside plastic screw top soda bottles.

Materials: juice can lids, jingle bells, pipe cleaners, dried beans, paper plates, stapler or tape, any size plastic soda bottles **Caution:** Rhythm band instruments should be stored out of reach when not in use.

Bat the Beach Ball

An inflatable beach ball is light enough for indoor play. Find a place to hang the ball from a basement rafter, a beam, or a wide door frame. Securely tape a sturdy string to the ball (another use for duct tape!). Suspend the ball so it hangs at her shoulder height. Now, she can swing at the ball and try to catch it as it swings back. You can substitute a balloon for the beach ball as long as this activity is supervised at all times. Deflated or popped balloon pieces are a serious choking hazard.

Developing Skills

- eye-hand coordination
- gross motor coordination

Variation: Bat a balloon in the air. Let her catch it, throw it, and bat it.

Materials: sturdy string, small beach ball, strong tape

Magnetic Fishing

Cut out several simple 4" (10 cm) fish shapes from different colors of construction paper. Clip a large metal paper clip on the end of each one. Attach a small magnet to one end of a piece of string about 12 inches long. Tie the other end to a "fishing pole" (wooden spoon, ruler, unsharpened pencil). Spread out all of the fish on the floor. Your toddler will be able to hook a fish by bringing the magnet close to the paper clip. As she catches each one, you can announce the color, "You caught a red fish. Now you caught a blue fish." **Variation:** Ask her to catch a fish of a certain color. Make the string longer to increase difficulty.

Materials: colored paper, paper clips, string, a ruler, magnet

Caution: Always put fish and clips away, out of reach, when not in use.

Developing Skills

- eye-hand coordination
- gross motor coordination
- concepts: color

Active Indoor Play

18 months and up

Bean Bag Game 1

Set an empty laundry basket in the middle of the room. Place a piece of tape on the floor a few feet away from the basket. Show your toddler how to toss the beanbags into the basket while she is standing behind the tape line. You can count the beanbags that went in and compare them to the beanbags that landed outside the basket. "One, two, three. Three bags are in the basket. One, two. Two bags are out." Put the beanbags in piles and ask which pile is bigger (smaller), or which pile has more (less). Encourage repetition to build skills.

Variations: Change the size of the target container. A shoebox or plastic bowl increases the difficulty. Move the target farther away from the tape line. Toss with different hands.

Materials: five bean bags or small stuffed animals, laundry basket, masking tape

Developing Skills

- gross motor exercise
- eye-hand coordination
- pre-math: exposure to counting

Storybook Extensions

Favorite stories will enable your toddler to integrate many skills through activities that incorporate repetition and movement. She learns powerful pre-literacy skills, including plot sequence, memory, patterns, rhyming and rhythm, and new vocabulary. Bring books to life with the following ideas or create some of your own. Choose a book very familiar to your child. For instance, *Where's Spot?* by Eric Hill. Make about five copies of Spot, the dog (photocopy or trace him on paper). Cut them out and mount them on cardboard to make them more durable. Now you can play *"Where's Spot?"* Place the pictures around the room. Give directions similar to the book's style. "Is he under the couch? Is he in the closet?" Let your toddler follow your directions to find them.

Materials: the book *Where's Spot?* by Eric Hill, thin cardboard, glue

Developing Skills

- pre-literacy
- imagination
- vocabulary enrichment

Storybook Extensions (cont.)

Using the book, *Brown Bear, Brown Bear, What Do You See?* by Bill Martin, Jr., play a game with your toddler, using homemade cards. Mount pictures of any animals from magazines on index cards or use animal flash cards. Lay five pictures in a row, face down. Have your toddler flip over the first card and say the chant from the book, "Cow, cow, what do you see?" Have her flip over the second card, "I see a lion looking at me." Repeat the pattern until all five animals have been revealed. For young toddlers, the fun will be in flipping the cards and naming the animals. Older children will be able to learn the pattern of the chant. They can practice memory skills by predicting which animal is next in the sequence of five cards on the second or third time through the activity.

Materials: animal flash cards or animal pictures glued on index cards, old magazines

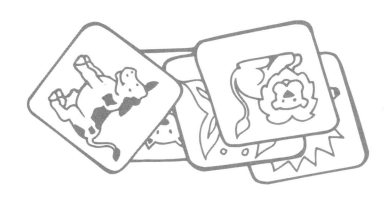

Developing Skills

- pre-literacy
- sequencing
- patterns

Hide and Seek 2

Gather a few of your toddler's small toys. Hide them around the living room. Now, sit down and ask him to "Find your truck." Give directions like, "Look under the chair," "Look behind the couch," "Look in the closet." After he brings the toy, ask, "Where was it?" To reinforce the preposition, repeat, "It was *under* the chair. You found the truck *under* the chair!"

Variations: The difficulty level can be changed by making items fully visible, partially visible, or completely hidden.

Materials: 3–4 small toys

Developing Skills

- receptive language
- memory
- purposeful movement

Streamers

Make a streamer to accompany movement to music. Having a focal point keeps the activity from getting out of control. Cut four or five 18" (45 cm) pieces of gift-wrap ribbon. Use different colors. Tape the strips to the end of a tongue depressor or craft stick. An empty toilet paper tube works, too. Decorate the stick with markers and stickers. Now when your toddler dances, he can wave the streamer around. Give him directions to follow, such as, "Wave your streamer high over your head. Shake it fast to the side. Twirl it in a circle. Wave it back and forth." **Variations:** Try using one streamer in each hand. Play different tempos of music, moving slowly or quickly as the music dictates. Does he respond to the beat? Play "Stop and Go" with the music.

Materials: ribbon, tape, craft sticks, markers, stickers, decorations

Developing Skills

- following directions
- social-emotional: self-control
- purposeful movement

Shake and Stop

Now that your toddler can stop and start his whole body to music, help him further refine his gross motor control by isolating one body part at a time. This can be done with or without music. Have him follow directions, "Shake until the music stops (or I say 'stop')." Give commands such as, "Shake your leg until the music stops." Now switch to "shake your arm, elbow, head, hips, etc."

Materials: radio or CD player

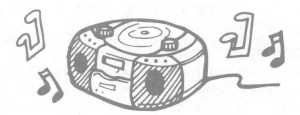

Developing Skills

- following directions
- social-emotional: self-control
- gross motor coordination

This Is the Way the Bunny Hops

Help your toddler learn different motor patterns such as hopping, galloping, crawling, and tiptoeing with this song, sung to the tune of "Here We Go Round the Mulberry Bush." Act out the motions with him.

This Is the Way the Bunny Hops

This is the way the bunny hops,
The bunny hops, the bunny hops.
This is the way the bunny hops.
So early in the morning.

Additional verses:

This is the way the turtle crawls, horse gallops, mouse tiptoes, bird flies, etc.

Developing Skills

- gross motor coordination
- pretend play

Happy and You Know It

Use this adaptation of the popular song to help your toddler learn to differentiate and identify feelings. You are also indirectly modeling appropriate ways to express feelings. Have him make faces to match the appropriate emotions.

Developing Skills

- social-emotional awareness
- gross motor coordination

If You're Happy and You Know It

If you're happy and you know it,
Give a smile,

If you're happy and you know it,
Give a smile,

If you're happy and you know it,
Then your face will surely show it.

If you're happy and you know it,
Give a smile.

Additional verses:

If you're angry; stomp your feet.
If you're sad; make a frown.
If you're excited; clap your hands,
If you're tired; yawn and stretch.

Active Indoor Play

24 months and up

Hammer and Nails

Create a realistic hammering activity with slabs of Styrofoam and golf tees as nails. Use a slab of two inch thick Styrofoam as a pounding board. You may need to glue two one-inch thick pieces together. Give your toddler a sturdy toy hammer or mallet. Let him pound golf tees into the Styrofoam. He can practice pulling the nails out with his fingers or with the claw end of the hammer.

Materials: wooden or plastic golf tees, hammer or mallet, a two-inch thick slab of Styrofoam about 12 inches square

Developing Skills

- pretend play
- eye-hand coordination
- gross motor coordination

Clap Your Hands Now

Developing Skills

- following directions
- body part awareness
- pre-math: one-to-one correspondence

Clap Your Hands Now

Sing this song to the tune of "Skip to My Lou." Do a few verses at first and then add more as your toddler learns them.

Clap your hands now, 1, 2, 3.
Clap your hands now, 1, 2, 3.

(Clap hands exactly three times as you count.)

Clap your hands now, 1, 2, 3.
Clap your hands, my darling.

Additional verses:

Stamp your feet, slap your knees,
tap your toes, nod your head,
pat your chest, blink your eyes.

Active Indoor Play

24 months and up

Color Hunt

Place a bright red sheet of paper on the floor. Now, walk through the house with your toddler looking for red objects. Place the objects on the red paper. Now, put a blue sheet next to the red paper. Help him search the house for blue objects. Bring them to the blue paper. Name each object, "The block is red. This car is red. These scissors are red," etc. Now, name all the blue objects. Now, mix the objects together and see if he can sort them by returning them to the right colored paper. For added memory exercise, see if he can put the items back where they were. Hold them up one at a time; "Where did we find this?" "Where does this go?"

Variations: Can he find items by himself? Can he sort three colors?

Materials: a sheet of red paper, a sheet of blue paper, household objects

Developing Skills

- sorting
- matching
- concepts: color

Bean Bag Game 2

Buy or make a few beanbags. Small beanbag animals work, too. You and your toddler can play this together. Push the beanbag across the carpet with one hand. Now pick a different body part to use in pushing the beanbag. Try your knee, nose, foot, or elbow. Once she understands the game, take turns picking the next body part.

Materials: beanbags

Developing Skills

- gross motor exercise
- body part identification

Bean Bag Game 3

Practice balance and body control with this activity. Show your toddler how to walk in a circle with a beanbag on her head. Accompany this activity with slow, relaxing music to help her focus on quieting her body. You can stop and start the walking as you stop and start the music to add listening skills to the game. Try having her balance the beanbag on different parts of the body: shoulder, back of the hand, forearm, or have her crawl on all fours with the beanbag on her back.

Variation: Combine this activity with "Walk the Line" on page 74.

Materials: one beanbag per person

Developing Skills

- gross motor exercise
- balance
- listening

Bean Bag Game 4

Stack six plastic cups in a pyramid formation on the floor. Have your toddler stand behind a tape line. Show her how to throw beanbags to knock down the cups. Because she doesn't understand numbers well enough yet to know that knocking them down with three bean bags is better than with five, let her use as many beanbags as necessary to complete the task. She will benefit from a sense of accomplishment. Besides, the more beanbags she uses, the more throwing she gets to do.

Variations: Adjust the difficulty by moving the target further away or by using more cups.

Materials: several bean bags, 6 plastic cups, masking tape

Developing Skills

- gross motor exercise
- eye-hand coordination

Walk the Line

Place a tape line across your kitchen floor. Show your toddler how to walk on the line by carefully placing one foot in front of the other. Let her follow you as you make your way along the tape. Give her a verbal cue, too, "My feet stay on the line." This activity requires the same skills as walking on a balance beam without the danger of falling off.

Variations: Try tiptoeing, or "brick stepping," by placing the heel of one foot up against the toe of the other as you go. Older children can try walking backwards.

Materials: masking tape

Developing Skills

- balance
- eye-foot coordination

Act Like an Animal

See if your toddler can create animal characteristics with body movement and sounds. Ask her to pretend she is a dog. Prompt her with, "Show me how a dog moves." "What does a dog say?" Now try another animal such as a snake, elephant, monkey, lion, or duck. A younger child may need to be shown some movements. See if she remembers them next time you play.

Materials: none

Developing Skills

- gross motor coordination
- pretend play

Acting 101

After an older toddler is very familiar with a story, try acting it out. She may enjoy dramatizing "The Three Bears." Include simple props like three bowls and spoons for the porridge, three chairs, and three pillows for the beds. You can narrate a simplified version of the story and prompt your child to act out the scenes. Maybe her teddy bears can help. Let her try different roles. The best ones are Baby Bear and Goldilocks (can be a boy or girl in your version). Try "The Three Little Pigs," Caps for Sale, or any other favorites.

Materials: add props as desired

Developing Skills

- pre-literacy: story sequence
- pretend play
- symbolic representation

Five Little Monkeys

In a safe, bouncy place, get some exercise and act out this poem with your toddler.

Five Little Monkeys

Five little monkeys jumping on the bed,
(Jump up and down while holding up five fingers.)

One fell off and bumped his head.
(Fall down and rub your head.)

**Momma called the doctor and
The doctor said,**
(Pantomime pushing phone buttons and holding the receiver to your ear.)

"No more monkeys jumping on the bed!"
(Waggle the finger of one hand with the other hand on hip.)

Additional verses: Continue counting down until no monkeys are left.

Developing Skills

- gross motor coordination
- pretend play

Head, Shoulders, Knees & Toes

Play this game either standing or sitting with legs outstretched. Start out by singing the song slowly enough that your toddler can keep up with the movements.

Head, shoulders, knees and toes,
Knees and toes.

(Touch each body part as you sing it throughout the song.)

Head, shoulders, knees and toes, knees and toes,
And eyes, and ears, and mouth and nose!

Say, "Now let's try it a little faster." Sing the song faster. Continue to repeat the song, each time saying, "Let's try it faster," until neither of you can keep up, you're mixing up body parts, and laughing. Then try it slower again.

Developing Skills

- gross motor coordination
- body part identification
- concepts: fast/slow

Advanced Head, Shoulders, Knees & Toes

Place a sticker on the back of your toddler's right hand. Place the same kind of sticker on her left shoulder, left knee, and left foot. Sing the song as usual but do the actions with just the right hand crossing over to touch the left side body parts. The stickers will target the spots for her. Play again with the stickers reversed so that she uses her left hand to touch the right side of her body.

Materials: colored dot stickers or star stickers

Developing Skills

- cross-lateral movement
- gross motor coordination
- body part identification

The Sensory Table Box

Toddlers love to dump and fill and dump again. Provide an acceptable area for this play by creating a sensory table. Use a plastic storage box with a top (such as an under-the-bed box). Place a vinyl tablecloth under the box to define the play space. Fill the box about one inch high with uncooked oatmeal. Collect scoops, small containers, and a dump truck to fill up and dump out. A funnel wheel is also a good investment. It will take vigilance to help your toddler learn to remain by the box. If he moves off the tablecloth take his toys out of his hands and redirect him either back to the box to continue to play, or to clean up. Shake the spilled oatmeal back into the box. **Variations:** Use puffed rice cereal, grits, uncooked rice, or dried lentils.

Materials: storage box, sand toys, vinyl tablecloth or shower curtain, dry oatmeal

Developing Skills

- tactile discrimination
- sensory exploration
- fine motor coordination
- spatial/temporal relationships

Sensory Table Washing

Toddlers like to feel purposeful. They show interest in real activities with real things. Put a fingernail brush and some apples in your sensory table. Add a few drops of mild soap. The brush is the right size for him to scrub the apples. As he finishes one, take it out and dry it with a dishtowel. (He may want to do this, too.) Wash another; dry it. You will reinforce the sequence of steps in the process each time you repeat it.

Variations: Use any durable fruit or veggie like carrots, winter squash, or oranges. Take the fun outside and wash other objects like muddy boots, rocks, or plastic toys. The dirtier, the better.

Materials: fingernail brush, mild soap, small towel

Developing Skills

- social-emotional: self-esteem
- fine motor coordination
- pre-literacy: sequencing a process

Sensory Table Math

Your toddler will free-play in the sensory table for some time. You can also use this play as an opportunity to introduce pre-math concepts to him. Make two piles of oats, rice, or lentils in the table. As you play, give lots of exposure to the words and the concepts of *less*, *more*, and *combined together*. Ask him which pile is *bigger*. Say, "Let's add *more* to this one, now it's even *bigger*." "Let's make a very *little* pile, this one has *less*." "Let's put these piles *together*, now we have one *huge* pile." "These piles are the *same*," etc.

Variations: Use water in the table along with various spoons, cups, and bowls. Use pre-math language like *full*, *empty*, *more*, *less*, *some*, *few*, during your play.

Materials: measuring cups and spoons, lentils, oats, or rice

Developing Skills

- pre-math concepts: mathematical groupings
- vocabulary enrichment
- fine motor coordination

First Play Dough

Play dough provides valuable sensory and fine motor experiences for your toddler. However, at this age he will likely want to put the dough in his mouth. The following recipe is non-toxic. You may want to add a strong flavor extract like coffee or almond to discourage him from eating the dough. Use play dough as a joint parent-and-child experience. With your supervision, he can explore and enjoy safely.

- 2¼ cups white flour
- ½ cup salt
- 2½ tsp. alum or cream of tartar*
- 2 cups boiling water
- 2 Tbsp. oil
- food coloring and flavor extracts as desired
- * alum and cream of tartar can be found in the spice section of the grocery store.

Combine dry ingredients in a bowl. Stir the liquids together before pouring into the bowl. Stir until mixture is too stiff; then knead with your hands until the dough is uniform and smooth. Play dough will last for weeks if it is stored in an airtight container, like a resealable plastic bag.

Play Dough Ideas

A good surface for using play dough is a plastic-coated place mat on a table. This also helps define a boundary for where the play dough is to stay and it makes the clean-up easier. When playing, always use rich language to complement your activities. Use such vocabulary words as *squishy, soft, squeeze, pull, poke,* and *stretch.*

Embed small toys in the dough. Let your toddler pull them out. Let him stick golf tees or pegs in the dough. Roll out a thin layer of dough. Have him drive toy cars across the dough to make tracks. Let him make impressions with kitchen utensils such as a potato masher, slotted spoon, plastic fork, etc. Knead in glitter to make the dough sparkly. Knead in sand or rice to change the texture. Let him snip apart thin ropes of play dough with scissors.

Materials: play dough, small toys, kitchen utensils

Developing Skills

- fine motor coordination
- sensory exploration
- vocabulary enrichment: attributes and verbs

Sponge Squeeze

Set up this activity at the kitchen table or high chair. Put two tablespoons of colored water in a saucer. Set a second saucer near the first. Show your toddler how to absorb the water with a little sponge. Where did the water go? Now for the fun part—show him how to squeeze the sponge over the second saucer. Surprise! Toddlers learn by watching. Repeat the process a few more times. Now, let your toddler experiment and practice transferring the liquid back and forth.

Materials: two small sponges (or cut one in half), shallow bowl or saucer, food coloring

Developing Skills

- eye-hand coordination
- fine motor coordination

Junk Mail

Make a mailbox by cutting a slot in the top of a shoebox. You can cover the box with blue wrapping paper and write MAIL on the front. Now, when the mail comes, your toddler can play with all the advertising circulars and junk mail offers. He can put them in his mailbox, take them out, and open the envelopes.

Materials: old shoebox, wrapping paper (optional), junk mail

Developing Skills

- eye-hand coordination
- fine motor coordination
- pretend play

Simple Puzzles

Mount pictures from magazines or extra photos on index cards or any stiff cardboard. Use a glue stick to make sure the entire surface is adhered. After they dry, cut the pictures into two pieces to make simple puzzles. Give your toddler two at a time. Can he find the missing halves?

Variations: Try matching three pairs of puzzle pieces. Cut a single picture into 3 or 4 pieces.

Materials: magazine pictures or photos, light cardboard, glue stick, scissors

Developing Skills

- cognitive: understanding part vs. whole
- cognitive: matching (non-identical parts)
- fine motor coordination

Go Fetch

Toddlers stay interested longer when movement is incorporated into activities. Choose five or six picture flash cards. Include words your toddler knows and one or two new ones. Label the pictures as you place them on the floor. Say, "This is a wagon. This is a giraffe," etc. Next, sit on the opposite side of the room and ask him to bring you a card. He gets to walk, turn, bend, and carry as he searches for the right card. If he brings the wrong one, just reinforce that one. "You brought a tiger. Can you find the giraffe?" If he brings you all of the correct cards, he knows those words. Add a few more new ones next time.

Variation: Set the cards all around the room. Your toddler must remember the location of each card.

Materials: picture flash cards

Developing Skills

- following directions
- receptive vocabulary: nouns
- memory

Mirror, Mirror on the Wall

Practice more than just your fairest face in the mirror. Bring your toddler to a mirror and show him a happy face. Ask him to copy it. Show him an angry face. Can he copy that one, too? Try others like *tired*, *sad*, *excited*, and *frightened*. Have him practice them all. Matching the face with the name of the emotion will help him become aware of his many feelings.

Materials: mirror

Developing Skills

- social-emotional: self-awareness
- imitation

Line Them Up

Toddlers like to put things in line. Put a length of masking tape on the floor or carpet. Now set a few blocks on the tape in single file. Your toddler will follow suit. She may enjoy lining up toy cars or shoes. Remove the tape before the adhesive sticks permanently to the floor. If you are willing to put a permanent mark on the floor, it will help your toddler know where her shoes go, either in her closet, or by the back door.

Variation: Try a tabletop version of this activity with a tape line and buttons or small blocks. Supervise this to ensure that your child doesn't put small objects in her mouth.

Materials: masking tape, small toys

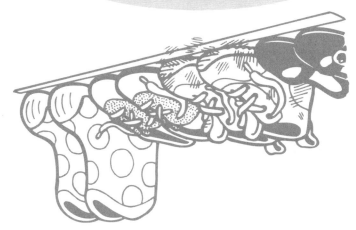

Developing Skills

- eye-hand coordination
- fine motor coordination

Stringing Beads

This stringing activity provides for lots of fine motor practice. Let your toddler string a variety of things to generate interest and encourage repetition. At first, try pipe cleaners (chenille sticks) as stringing material. She will be able to more easily manipulate them. Plastic-coated wire also works well. String beads, macaroni noodles, large paperclips, spools, or anything with a hole in it. The smaller the hole, the greater her challenge. To make string or yarn easier to work with, dip the end (about one inch/2.5 cm) in glue. After it is dry, the stiffness makes it easier to thread.

Developing Skills

- eye-hand coordination
- fine motor coordination

Variation: Make an edible necklace with shoestring licorice and loop cereal.

Materials: pipe cleaners, string, beads, macaroni

Car Wash

Set up this activity in your sensory table box (see page 80) to minimize the mess. Squirt a small pile of foamy shaving cream in one end of the box. Put a shallow bowl of water in the center. Lay a small dishtowel at the other end. Now your toddler can wash her toy cars. She can drive her cars through the foam and smear it around. She can dip them in the water to rinse and then dry them with the towel. Let her free-play or do one car at a time to sequence a three-step process.

Materials: foamy shaving cream, bowl of water, small towel, toy cars

Developing Skills

- pre-literacy: sequencing
- sensory motor play
- pretend play

More Sensory Table Ideas

After your toddler no longer automatically puts things in her mouth, try the following ideas. Renew interest in pouring, scooping, and measuring by changing what's in the sensory table. Try uncooked pasta (wheels, elbows, or twists), mixed birdseed, packing peanuts, marbles, shredded paper, dried kidney beans, or colored aquarium gravel. She can explore the different properties of each material, its weight, density, texture, how well it pours and stacks, etc. Include small toys to hide and uncover, little trucks to drive, etc. Hide several small stones, including one painted gold. Look for the "Golden Nugget." You and your toddler can take turns hiding it for each other.

Materials: various

Developing Skills

- vocabulary enrichment: attributes
- exploration and experimentation
- pre-math concepts: heavy and light

Tong Transfer 1

The fine motor squeeze-and-release movements in this activity prepare your toddler's hand for cutting with scissors. Use sugar cube tongs or some other small tongs. Set out one small bowl with five little pompons in it. Set an empty bowl to the right of the first. Show her how to pick up a pompon with the sugar tongs and transfer it to the empty bowl. Encourage her to try it once with each hand, but always demonstrate the transfer left to right. Your toddler may transfer back and forth.

Developing Skills

- pre-literacy: left to right orientation
- eye-hand coordination
- fine motor skills

Materials: small squeeze-operated tongs like sugar tongs, toast tongs, or a strawberry huller, small pompons proportionate to the tong size you have, two bowls

Pitcher to Pitcher

Let your toddler practice pouring with her right and left hands. Using two small pitchers, fill one half full. Add a few drops of food coloring to tint the water. This makes it easier to see. She can pour the water back and forth between the pitchers. As her skill improves, fill the pitcher three quarters full. You can set this activity up on a cookie sheet so any spills are contained. Let her use a little sponge to wipe those.

Materials: two small pitchers, one-cup liquid measuring cups with a spout and handle

Developing Skills

- eye-hand coordination
- independence
- social-emotional: self-help skills

Matching

Matching, one of your toddler's earliest cognitive abilities, involves recognizing *same* and *different*. First, try visual matching with identical pairs of objects that differ from one another by more than one attribute. Little yellow stars, big red circles, and medium blue squares differ in color, size, and shape. Place three pairs of objects randomly in front of your toddler. Hold up one and ask her to hand you the one that looks just like it. As she learns to follow the directions and play along, increase the difficulty by making the objects more similar.

Variations: Involve other senses. Use touch by matching textures of sandpaper. Dip your toddler's fingers in cups of warm or cold water. Can she match by temperature?

Materials: various pairs of identical objects

Developing Skills

- concepts: size, shape, or color
- cognitive: matching
- following directions

Sorting

A divided plastic picnic plate with one big section and two equal smaller sections makes a good sorting surface. Lacking that, you could use a big bowl and two little bowls instead. Mix five identical big buttons and five identical little buttons in the big section. Show your toddler how to sort by putting the big buttons in one of the small sections and the little ones in the other. You will be sorting by only one attribute and that is size. Comment on the size of each one as she sorts, "Here's a big one; it goes here. This is a little button; it goes here."

Developing Skills

- concepts: size, shape, or color
- cognitive: sorting
- fine motor coordination

Variations: Sort by another single attribute. Try color, using colorful candies or different colored cotton balls. Try sorting by shape with little square crackers and round ones, or checkers and dominoes.

Materials: divided plate, large and small buttons

What Does It Feel Like?

Place a well-known object in a cloth bag or adult-size sock. See if your toddler can identify it by feel alone without peeking. Remove it from the bag to see if her guess is correct. Try another object. It may be hard to fool her after a few tries. This game builds the ability to form a picture in the mind's eye.

Materials: several small objects: a spoon, a pencil, a key, a block, etc.

Developing Skills

- pre-literacy: visual memory
- cognitive: object recognition
- by touch
- fine motor coordination

Nuts and Bolts

Toddlers like to use real objects. Buy a few large bolts and some nuts to thread on them. At first, give her two or three that are all the same size. The challenge here is to thread the nut on the bolt. Increase the challenge by giving her two smaller bolts and nuts. Now, she must find the corresponding nut for each bolt.

Materials: various sizes of nuts and corresponding bolts

Developing Skills

- matching
- sorting
- fine motor coordination

Gloop

Developing Skills

- sensory motor play
- exploration and discovery

Mix one box of cornstarch with enough water to make a thin paste. Tint the mixture with food coloring if desired. Place the Gloop in a 9" x 13" (23 cm x 33 cm) pan in order to contain it. Prepare a space for your toddler to play with Gloop (on a plastic or vinyl placemat, for instance). Give him some plastic spoons, little cups, forks, etc. Allow him to experiment with it. Show him how to put some in his hand and squeeze it. The Gloop sometimes feels wet, sometimes dry. It changes from thick to thin as it is stirred. This stuff cleans up easily. After it dries, just brush off the powder.

Materials: cornstarch, baking pan, water, (optional: food coloring)

Glurch

Developing Skills

- sensory motor play
- exploration and discovery

This concoction is stickier and messier than Gloop, but well worth the experience for your toddler. Mix equal parts of washable white school glue with liquid starch in a bowl. A half cup of each makes a manageable amount. Hand mixing it is half the fun. Spoon a little directly on a plastic place mat in front of your toddler. Show him that this stuff oozes and drips if pulled slowly and snaps apart if pulled quickly. You can embed small plastic toy animals in it and have him find them. The Glurch sort of sticks, but peels off. Add more starch if it gets too sticky. (If any gets on clothing, soak in a bucket of water to dissolve the glue and launder as usual.) Store in a tightly covered container or resealable plastic bag.

Materials: liquid starch, available in the laundry supply section at the supermarket, washable white school glue

Eye Droppers

This activity allows for further refinement of your toddler's squeeze-and-release grasp. It uses just his thumb and first two fingers (the same ones used when holding a pencil). Pour a quarter of a cup of water into each of three little bowls. With food coloring, tint one bowl of water dark red, one dark blue, and one dark yellow. Glass or white bowls show the colors best. Put an eyedropper in each bowl. Show your toddler how to drip two colors into a fourth bowl. Notice the color change. Pour the mix out and try two other colors. Experiment!

Variation: Drip the colors onto a clean white coffee filter or a thick, folded paper towel. The colors will run together and mix. Let it dry.

Materials: four small bowls, three eye droppers, food coloring, coffee filters or paper towels

Developing Skills

- fine motor coordination
- exploration and discovery

Write and Squish

Place about two tablespoons of catsup in a sandwich-size resealable plastic bag. Squeeze out the excess air and seal. Tape the bag onto a table. Show your toddler how to use his index finger to press down on the bag and draw lines. Squish and pat the bag to erase the marks. Make two bags so you can demonstrate a shape or letter for him to copy. Try a circle, a cross, a "T." Allow time for him to experiment freely.

Materials: catsup, resealable bags, tape

Developing Skills

- fine motor coordination
- pre-writing: copying shapes
- creativity

Tong Transfer 2

This version of transferring with tongs requires more control from your toddler than the activity on page 94. Kitchen tongs don't have the springy release built in. Place some cotton balls on a table in front of him and to one side of an empty egg carton. Let him pick up the cotton balls and transfer them into the egg carton. This activity reinforces left-to-right orientation. He may need to use two hands to control the tongs until his hands get bigger. Twelve balls, twelve holes. That's one-to-one correspondence.

Materials: twelve cotton balls, an empty egg carton, kitchen tongs

Developing Skills

- pre-math: one-to-one correspondence
- eye-hand coordination
- fine motor coordination

Memory Recall

Place four small objects on a tray. Cover them all with a towel. Remove the towel and name each object with your toddler. Now cover them again. See how many he can remember without peeking.

Variations: Reach under the towel and remove one object. Uncover the tray and see if he can name the missing object. Increase the number of objects to increase the difficulty. Reverse the roles and let your toddler remove an object for you to guess.

Materials: a tray, a hand towel, and small household items such as a spoon, a pencil, a rubber band, a paper clip, a coin, a button, etc.

Developing Skills

- pre-literacy: visual memory
- social-emotional: taking turns

Matching by Sound

Make a sound matching game for your toddler with empty plastic film canisters. Start with four canisters. Fill two of them half way with salt. Fill the other two half way with dried beans. All four look the same, but there are two identical pairs that match by the sound they make when shaken. Shake the canisters one at a time with your toddler, "This one is loud." "This one is quiet." "Here's another quiet one," etc. Now ask him to find the one that matches the one that you are shaking. After both pairs are found, mix them up and see if your toddler can do it all by himself. **Variations:** Add another pair by putting uncooked rice in two more canisters. Change what is in the canisters from time to time to renew interest in the activity.

Materials: six empty film canisters, salt, rice, dried beans

Developing Skills

- cognitive: matching
- pre-literacy: sound discrimination
- vocabulary enrichment: loud, quiet

Matching by Taste

Give your toddler another kind of matching experience by involving his sense of taste. Put a little honey or maple syrup in a cup. Put orange juice in another. Seat your toddler at a table. He will need to close his eyes for this. Use a spoon to put a drip of syrup on his tongue. Can he identify the substance? Now give him a taste of the juice. Is it the same or different? Can he match the tastes as you give him repeated trials?

Variation: Add a third flavor. Make the distinction between the flavors less noticeable. For example have him try to tell the difference between apple and pear juice.

Materials: flavorful liquids like maple syrup, fruit juices, and honey

Developing Skills

- cognitive: matching
- taste discrimination
- vocabulary enrichment: *sweet*, *tangy*, *sour*, *fruity*

Puppet Theater

Make a simple puppet theater for your toddler with a spring-operated shower curtain pole. Hang the pole across a doorway at his shoulder height. Drape a sheet over it. He can use puppets or stuffed animals to put on a show. Suggest that one of the puppets sing a song. You can interview an animal puppet with simple questions such as, "What is your name?" "What do you eat?" and "Where do you live?" Make simple stick puppets by photocopying storybook characters from pages of favorite books. Mount them on craft sticks and act out well-known stories.

Materials: spring-loaded shower curtain pole, sheet, puppets or stuffed animals

Developing Skills

- pre-literacy: retelling a story
- imagination
- pretend play

Patterning

Developing Skills

- cognitive: seeing and copying patterns
- fine motor coordination

An important cognitive skill for reading and math involves recognizing patterns. There are patterns in music, language, body movements, behaviors, and routines. Help your toddler identify visual patterns with these ideas. Lay out a simple pattern with coins in a row: penny, nickel, penny, nickel, etc. See if he can copy the pattern by making a row right next to yours. Make another pattern and see if he can tell you what comes next. You may need to label and point to the pattern to help him recognize the pattern. Make other patterns using small blocks, shapes cut from colored paper or felt, paper clips, and safety pins, etc.

Variations: Increase the difficulty of the pattern by adding a third element or try a more intricate pattern with two elements: ABCABCABC or ABBABBABB.

Materials: 10 pennies, 10 nickels

Introduction to Simple Art

Early art experiences involve the senses (the feel of fingerpaint), cause-and-effect relationships (glue makes things stick, crayons leave marks), sequencing a process, and learning how to use the art materials. Toddlers enjoy exploring the different properties (sticky glue, wet paint, squeezable dough) of various mediums. These new experiences give you the opportunity to introduce the corresponding vocabulary words.

Toddler artwork is not representational at this point. They enjoy the exploration and process more than the product, so don't worry about how it "turns out." You're lucky if a toddler spends five minutes on one activity. Encourage your toddler's efforts with comments like, "I see a lot of blue right here, and there's a little yellow squiggle."

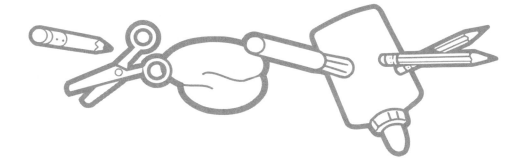

Introduction to Simple Art (cont.)

Describing what you see in the artwork is better than asking what it is. You don't need to save or display all their works. Use the best as wrapping paper, or cut out a shape to make a greeting card for someone special.

Keep a variety of art supplies on hand, but out of your toddler's reach. Colored papers, scissors, and crayons are staples. Look for washable, non-toxic paints, glue, markers, and ink pads. Know that art is messy business. Prepare an area by putting newspaper on the table and floor. Dress your toddler and yourself in old clothes that can get stained and paint-covered. If you prefer, you can move the entire operation outside and save yourself some cleanup.

Finger Paint Pudding

This messy activity is perfect for the high chair. Prepare vanilla instant pudding as directed. Spoon it into three different cups. Add a different food coloring to each cup. Now place a dollop of each color on your toddler's high chair tray. Let her squish and smear the pudding. Watch the colors mix. If you like, you can make a print of her design by pressing a sheet of paper on the tray. Peel it up to reveal the masterpiece.

Materials: one package of instant vanilla pudding, food coloring

Developing Skills

- fine motor coordination
- sensory motor play
- concepts: color

Toddler Crayons

Make thick crayons that don't break easily, are easy to hold, and won't fit in your toddler's mouth. Using a microwave, melt regular crayons in a glass dish lined with waxed paper. It may take several minutes; check and stir often. Or, place the crayons in a glass or plastic dish in a sunny spot (check from time to time—it will take a while). Spoon the melted crayons into the slots of an ice cube tray. Let them cool and harden. Allow your toddler to hold her crayon any way she wants to. This motor coordination, combined with the realization that the moving crayon is making that colored mark is enough of a challenge for toddlers. Just let her enjoy the scribbling process.

Materials: crayons with paper removed, ice cube trays, glass dish, waxed paper, plastic spoon

Developing Skills

- gross motor coordination
- fine motor coordination
- cause and effect

Introducing Markers

Cover a table with large paper such as butcher paper or newsprint. Keep the markers out of your toddler's reach in a high cupboard. Bring them out when you can supervise and guide their use. Keep the caps away; they are choking hazards. Show her how to scribble with a marker. Offer one and identify the color. Trade another color for the one she has. Let her draw with either hand. Here is your chance to reinforce that we only draw on appropriate surfaces. This can be one of those activities that you pull out when you need to be on the telephone. She can color; you can supervise.

Variation: Can she reach across her midline (across body) to draw a continuous line from the far left side to the far right side?

Materials: water-soluble markers, large paper

Developing Skills

- cross-lateral coordination
- vocabulary enrichment: color names
- understanding limits

Glue Stick

A non-toxic, water-soluble glue stick is a great first experience with glue for your toddler. Get the kind that is tinted so the glue shows up on the paper. She may think this is a lipstick, at first. You will need to demonstrate how it works. Dab a bit of glue on a piece of paper. Stick on a scrap of paper or fabric. Repeat the process, reinforcing the sequence with a verbal cue like: "Dab and stick. Dab and stick." Let her experiment.

Materials: glue stick, snippets of tissue paper, construction paper, fabric pieces

Developing Skills

- fine motor coordination
- two-step process/sequencing
- how to glue

Color Squish

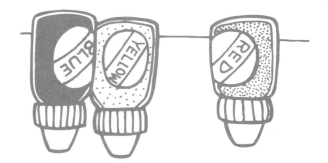

Mix a blob of hair gel with a little blue food coloring. Tint a second blob yellow. Put both blobs in a sandwich bag, keeping them separated. Now let your toddler squeeze and poke the bag. Notice and name the colors as she mixes them. Let her try it with red and yellow food coloring.

Materials: colorless hair gel, food coloring, sandwich-size resealable plastic bag

Developing Skills

- fine motor coordination
- concepts: color
- vocabulary enrichment: color names

Suncatcher

Cut two 5" (13 cm) circles from clear shelf paper. Let your toddler place sequins, confetti, glitter, foil, etc., on one of the circles. Use the second circle to cover and seal the first. Poke a little hole at the top and hang this in a sunny window. Remember, the best time to teach new words is when she is experiencing them. Build her vocabulary with words like *sticky*, *shiny*, *sparkle*, etc.

Variation: Help your toddler make a collage, on clear shelf paper, of found objects from a nature walk (leaves, twigs, pebbles, petals, feathers).

Materials: clear shelf paper, bits of paper, sequins, and glitter

Developing Skills

- vocabulary enrichment: attributes
- eye-hand coordination
- creativity

Texture Rubbings

Peel the paper off a thick crayon or use a homemade one from page 113. Lay a piece of smooth paper over a textured surface. Show your toddler how to lay the crayon on its side and rub on the paper. It takes some coordination for him to be able to rub hard enough. The texture beneath will leave a design on the paper. With your toddler, look for different textures around the house such as a tiled floor, raised design wallpaper, wood grain, etc. When he has finished, use the paper as wrapping paper, or cut it to make a card to send to Grandma. She'll love it.

Materials: crayons, thin paper

Developing Skills

- eye-hand coordination
- fine motor coordination
- vocabulary enrichment: attributes

Stamping

Purchase water-soluble ink pads and stamps at a specialty toy store. Your toddler will have to learn how to press first on the ink pad then on the paper. He will learn this best by watching you repeat the process slowly. Let him freely stamp on paper. Maybe you could make it into stationery.

Variation: Divide a piece of paper into 2" squares. Show your toddler how to stamp inside the squares on the divided paper. Increase the difficulty with smaller stamps and smaller squares.

Materials: ink pad, assorted stamps, paper

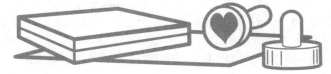

Developing Skills

- eye-hand coordination
- creativity with designs and patterns
- pre-math: one-to-one correspondence

Simple Art

24 months and up

Liquid Glue

There is a delayed cause and effect with liquid glue. You have to wait until it dries to show your toddler what it does. Tape a paper plate to a table. Pour about a tablespoon of glue in the center of the plate. Demonstrate for your toddler the simple two-step process, dip and stick. Have him dip packing peanuts or cotton balls in the glue and stick them to sturdy paper. If you wish, you can cut out a simple sheep shape ahead of time for the cotton balls.

Variation: Have your toddler dip cookie cutters in the glue to make outline shapes on the paper. Shake on glitter. This makes nice wrapping paper.

Materials: washable white glue, cotton balls or packing peanuts, paper plate, sturdy paper

Developing Skills

- creativity with designs and patterns
- sequencing a two-step process
- eye-hand coordination

Scissors Snip

Set up a successful first experience with scissors for your toddler with this idea. Prepare several strips of paper about one inch wide by six inches long. Hold a strip taut in front of your child. All he needs is one snip to see that the strip is cut in two. Hold up one of the cut pieces for him to cut again. The immediate success may spur him on to cut all the strips you prepared. Save those snippets for a glue stick collage project.

Variations: Let your toddler hold the strip while he cuts. Make the strips wider.

Materials: child-size scissors, strips of paper

Developing Skills

- eye-hand coordination
- fine motor skills
- independence/self-help skills

Leaving Tracks

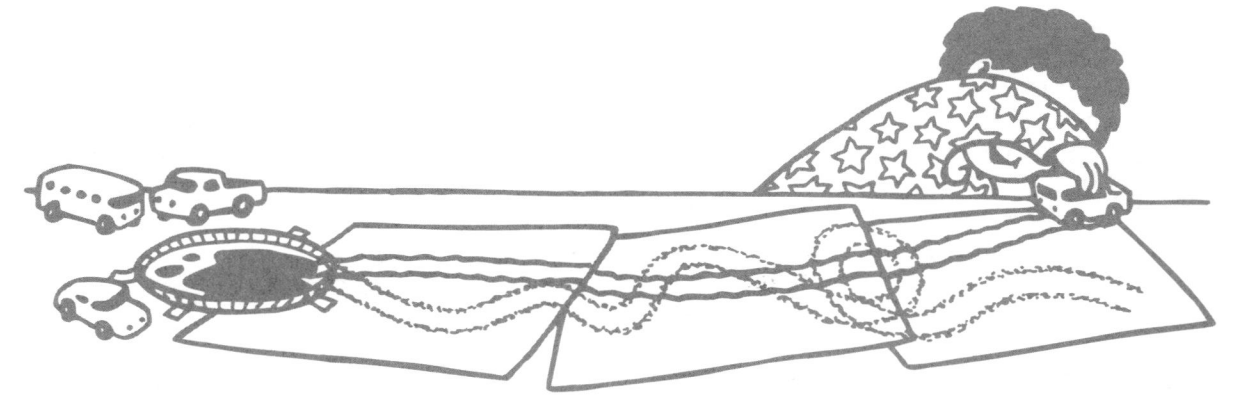

Developing Skills

- eye-hand coordination
- creativity with designs and patterns

Tape a paper plate to a table. Spread about two tablespoons of washable paint on it. Let your toddler drive a plastic car through the paint and then drive it on paper. Let him try other vehicles to make different designs.

Materials: paper plate, paint, plastic cars

Golf Ball Painting

Lay a sheet of paper in a 9" by 13" (23 cm x 33 cm) cake pan or large box top. Submerge a golf ball in a jar of paint. Fish it out with a fork or slotted spoon and place it in the pan. Let your toddler tip the pan to make the ball roll all over the paper. Add another ball with another color, if you wish.

Materials: paint, golf balls, oblong cake pan, paper

Developing Skills

- eye-hand coordination
- cause and effect
- creativity with designs and patterns

Copy with Markers

See how much control your toddler has gained by trying this every once in a while. Ask your toddler to watch you draw something. Make a short horizontal line on paper. Ask him to trace over it with his marker. Can he follow the direction and approximate length? Try a vertical line next. How about a circle?

Variation: In addition to more complex figures like zigzags or loops, try having your toddler copy, on his own, without tracing, the lines you make.

Materials: markers and paper

Developing Skills

- eye-hand coordination
- pre-visual discrimination of shapes

Gingerbread Boy

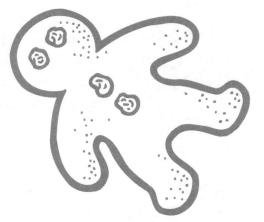

Cut a simple gingerbread boy figure out of sandpaper. Let your toddler vigorously rub a cinnamon stick across it. It will smell yummy. Glue on raisins for features like eyes or buttons. This makes a cute Christmas tree ornament or a good prop for dramatizing the gingerbread boy story.

Materials: sandpaper, a whole cinnamon stick, raisins, glue

Developing Skills

- fine motor coordination
- sense of smell

Painting with Glue

In a paper cup, thin two parts glue with one part water. Add a few drops of food coloring to make the glue easier to see. Give your toddler a small paintbrush to spread the glue on the paper. She can free-design at first. Sprinkle the wet paper with sand, sawdust, dry coffee grounds, or glitter. Shake off the excess to reveal her design.

Variation: Show her how to paint glue on the outlines of a simple picture from a coloring book. This tracing requires a lot of fine motor control.

Materials: glue, small paint brush, sand or glitter, paper, food coloring, paper cup, water, sawdust, dry coffee grounds

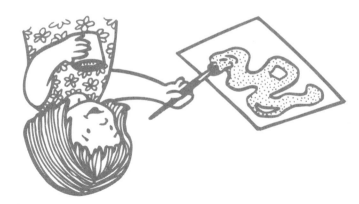

Developing Skills

- eye-hand coordination
- sequencing a two-step process
- creativity with designs and patterns

Blot Painting

Fold a piece of construction paper in half. Cut a simple shape like a heart or butterfly from the construction paper. Lay the shape flat. Let your toddler sqeeze the paint bottle and drip a few drops of paint, in two colors, on the fold. (Note: Sqeezing and stopping are tricky at first.) Now close the paper at the fold and have her press and slide her hands over the paper. Open the paper to reveal a Rorschach-like ink blot design. Add more paint if desired.

Materials: construction paper, paint in squirt bottles, scissors

Developing Skills

- fine motor coordination
- creativity with designs and patterns

Printing with Food

Slice an orange in half. Let it drain, cut side down, on a paper towel. Tape a paper plate to the table. Spread about two tablespoons of washable paint on the plate. Show your toddler how to dip the orange in the paint and make prints on paper. Try this with a cut apple.

Variations: Slice a potato in half. Cut designs in the potato's surface. Have your toddler press the potato half in paint and then onto paper. Spread a thin layer of paint on the vein side of a freshly picked leaf. Help your toddler press it on a sheet of paper. Experiment with a variety of leaf types and shapes.

Materials: paint, paper, an orange or apple, tape

Put It All Together

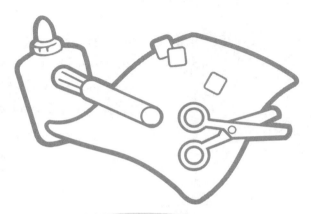

Now that your toddler has experience with glue, markers, stamps, and scissors, create a project that requires the use of any combination of skills.

Make a mosaic design: Have her snip apart strips of different colored construction paper. Now she can "dab and stick" with a glue stick. She can arrange the snippets on a sheet of black paper.

Stained glass design: Have your toddler snip colored tissue paper and glue it on waxed paper or Mylar to let light shine through.

Stamp, color, cut, glue: After she has stamped designs on ruled paper (see page 119), let her color the designs with markers. Now, let her cut and glue the pieces on a bigger sheet of paper.

Materials: various art supplies

Developing Skills

- pre-literacy: sequencing a 3 or 4-step process
- creativity with designs and patterns
- cutting, pasting, drawing

Animal Headbands

These simple headbands are fun for your toddler to decorate and are a great addition to imaginative play.

Bear: Cut two 3" (8 cm) strips from a 9" x 12" (23 cm x 30 cm) sheet of brown construction paper. Piece them together with tape or staples to make one long strip. Fit it to size around her head. Use the extra paper to make round ears. Draw eyes and a nose.

Pig: Use pink paper to make the headband. Make rounded triangular ears and a circular snout. Add a curly paper tail.

Spider: Use black paper. Cut eight thin strips for the legs. Attach them to the top edge of the headband so they drape downward.

Materials: construction paper, scissors, tape, markers

Developing Skills

- imagination
- pretend play
- cutting, pasting, drawing

Salt Dough

Your toddler can make Christmas ornaments or refrigerator magnets from this sturdy dough. With your toddler, mix together 4 cups of white flour and 1 cup of salt. Stir in 1½ cups of water and mix until smooth. Have her knead the dough by hand. Refrigerate overnight. Roll the dough out on a floured surface to about ¼ inch thick. Give her cookie cutters to cut the dough to make a variety of shapes. Using a toothpick, poke holes in the top of the creations to make hanging decorations. Bake for 1½ hours at 300° F. After they have cooled completely, have your toddler paint them. Glue a small magnet on the back for a refrigerator magnet.

Materials: 4 cups flour, 1 cup salt, water, toothpicks, cookie cutters, small magnets or sticky-back magnetic tape, acrylic paints

Developing Skills

- fine motor coordination
- pre-math
- creativity with designs and patterns

Homemade Stickers

Cut pictures from glossy magazines. Make a special glue as follows. Mix one packet of unflavored gelatin (about one tablespoon) with one tablespoon of water in a microwavable cup. Microwave on high for 30 seconds. Stir until melted and smooth. With your toddler, spread the glue on the backs of the magazine pictures with a little paintbrush. Let them dry thoroughly. Store them on waxed paper. To use the stickers, have her moisten them with a damp sponge and adhere on plain paper.

Materials: unflavored gelatin, water, glossy pictures, paintbrush, scissors

Developing Skills

- fine motor coordination
- creativity

Sandwich Shapes

Place a slice of cheese or meat on a piece of bread. Let your toddler choose a cookie cutter shape to press through the sandwich. Coat the cookie cutter with non-stick spray or dip in flour to prevent sticking.

Materials: bread slices, slices of cheese and/or meat, cookie cutter

Developing Skills

- fine motor coordination
- social-emotional: making choices

133

18 months and up

Cheese Cubes

Arrange six small cubes of cheese on a plate with six pretzel sticks. Show your toddler how to insert the pretzel sticks into the cheese. By matching the same number of cubes and sticks, he is exposed to one-to-one correspondence.

Materials: cheese cut in small cubes, pretzel sticks

Developing Skills

- fine motor coordination
- pre-math exposure

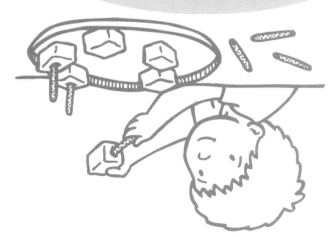

Snack Mix

Your toddler will get lots of practice scooping, filling, pouring, and emptying with this activity. *Many*, *few*, *more*, *some*, *less*, *empty*, and *full* are early math concepts. Set out boxes of various snack foods like little cheese crackers, soy nuts, raisins, mini marshmallows, and shaped cereals (o's, squares, balls). Let him scoop out one of each with a ¼ cup measuring spoon into a large bowl. Let him stir them before scooping the mix into single serving containers or little plastic bags. Eating finger foods is fine motor practice.

Developing Skills

- fine motor coordination
- pre-math concepts: mathematical groupings

Materials: various dry cereals, small pretzels, soy nuts, etc.

Recipes for Fun

18 months and up

Ants on a Log

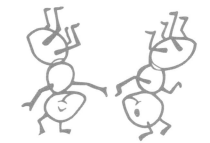

With prepared celery sticks, fill the groove with the spread of your choice (soy butter, apple butter, hummus, etc.). Let your toddler place the "ants" (raisins or soy nuts) on the spread.

Materials: celery stalks, washed and cut into 4" (10 cm) sticks, apple butter, soy butter, or mild hummus, raisins or soy nuts

Developing Skills

- fine motor coordination
- symbolic representation
- imagination

Soy Butter Play Dough

Your toddler can roll, pinch, sculpt, and finally, eat this dough. Have your toddler help mix all of the ingredients together. Adjust the consistency by altering the amount of powdered milk.

Materials:

4 Tbsp. soy butter

2 Tbsp. maple syrup

2½ Tbsp. powdered milk or soy powdered milk

Developing Skills

- fine motor coordination
- sensory motor play
- pre-math

Merry-Go-Rounds

Spread cream cheese or soy butter on cored apple slices. Or let your toddler try spreading it herself with a plastic butter knife. Now she can stand 3–4 animal crackers around the ring to make a merry-go-round.

Materials: one apple, cored and sliced in rounds, soy butter or cream cheese, animal crackers

Developing Skills

- fine motor coordination
- imagination

Rainbow Toast

Put a small amount of milk or soymilk into three cups. Add a little food coloring to each cup. Using paintbrushes, have your toddler decorate the bread. Toast the bread in a toaster oven or broiler. Do not use a regular toaster.

Materials: brand new little paintbrushes (washed and reserved just for food activities), light bread slices, milk, food coloring

Developing Skills

- fine motor coordination
- imagination

Gone Fishin'

Place a dollop of soy butter or apple butter on a plate with stick pretzels and fish crackers. Show your toddler how to dip one end of the pretzel (fishing pole) in the spread (bait) and catch a fish by pressing the pretzel end to the cracker.

Materials: stick pretzels, soy butter or apple butter, fish crackers

Developing Skills

- fine motor coordination
- symbolic representation
- imagination

Snack in a Jar

Give your toddler a little extra incentive to work at removing lids with this idea. Place her snacks in a few plastic jars. Let her figure out how to unscrew those lids.

Materials: clean plastic containers like peanut butter jars, yogurt cups, screw-top bottles, etc., finger-food snacks like carrot sticks, small crackers, cereal

Developing Skills

- fine motor coordination
- problem solving

Monkey Milk

Let your toddler peel a banana. You may need to crack the peel at the stem end to start it for her. Let your toddler slice the banana with a small butter knife. She may enjoy the slicing so much that she cuts it into tiny pieces. Put the pieces in the blender and add milk or soymilk. Let your toddler do as much as she can, pouring the milk in, pushing the ON button, etc. Accomplishments like this build confidence. There is enough Monkey Milk for both of you to enjoy.

Materials: one ripe banana, two cups milk or soy/rice milk, small butter knife, blender

Developing Skills

- fine motor coordination
- social-emotional: self-help skills

Sailboats

The real value in food activities is letting your child do as much of the process as he can. When there are multiple steps, the child learns sequencing and memory. You can enhance this by asking questions each time you make a snack in the future: "What will we need to make these? What do we do first? What comes next?"

Cut celery stalks into four-inch sections. Have your toddler help you fill them with spread. Show him how a pretzel stick can be a mast. Cut a cheese slice diagonally to make two triangles. Carefully poke the mast through the cheese sails and then stand it up in the spread.

Materials: celery stalks, soy butter or cream cheese, processed cheese slices, pretzel sticks

Developing Skills

- cognitive: sequencing
- fine motor coordination
- social-emotional: self-help skills

Banana Rounds

Let your older toddler peel and cut a firm banana into several slices. With practice, he will get better at making them almost the same size. Now count the slices, pointing to each one as you say the number. Next, count out the same number of round crackers and lay them in a row. Have your toddler place one banana slice on each cracker while you count. He will be very proud to hold the plate and serve these as appetizers to the whole family.

Variation: Peel and slice a hard boiled egg. Substitute for the banana slices.

Materials: one banana, several round crackers, small plastic knife

Developing Skills

- one-to-one correspondence
- fine motor coordination
- social-emotional: self-help skills

Frozen Banana Pops

Developing Skills

- one-to-one correspondence
- fine motor coordination
- social-emotional: self-help skills

Cut each banana in half width-wise. Count the halves out loud with your toddler. Count out eight sticks. Let your toddler match a stick to each banana. Insert a stick into each of the cut ends. Freeze until firm. Help him notice what happened to the bananas; they are now cold and firm. Heat the shortening over low heat; add chips and stir until smooth. Remove from heat. Have your toddler help place the granola in a shallow pan. Dip frozen bananas in the chocolate and let him roll them in granola to coat. Place them on waxed paper and freeze. Wrap individually in plastic to store.

Materials:

1 cup granola

1 cup chocolate chips

8 wooden frozen dessert sticks

2 tsp shortening

4 firm bananas

Recipes for Fun

30 months and up

Collage Sandwiches

Let your child use his imagination to create faces or designs on open-faced sandwiches. Spread cream cheese or mild hummus on a slice of bread. Add details with a variety of ingredients, for example: coconut or grated carrot for hair or fur; raisins for eyes; strips of lunchmeat or pickles for the mouth; cucumber or carrot rounds for noses, ears, or, the wheels of a car, etc.

Materials: bread, cream cheese or hummus, various sandwich ingredients

Developing Skills

- imagination
- fine motor coordination
- social-emotional: self-help skills

Fruit Kabobs

Pull together a few skills with this activity. Let your toddler peel and slice a banana. If you cut a thin rod of cheese, he can cut that into cubes. He could also cut pear or apple slices into chunks. Include grapes and canned pineapple chunks. Assemble all the cut food on a large plate. Provide your toddler with wooden shish kabob skewers. Let him poke the food onto the skewers. Ask him to copy your pattern. Try an ABAB pattern like apple, cheese, apple, cheese. Ask him to make a pattern for you to copy. Make the patterns more complex as his skills grow. Remember to include him in the cleanup. Of course, everyone gets to eat the kabobs when you're finished.

Materials: shish kabob skewers, cut fruits and cheeses, small plastic knife

Developing Skills

- fine motor coordination
- social-emotional: self-help skills
- pre-math: recognizing and forming patterns

Homemade Apple Sauce

Peel and core one apple. Cut it into several thin slices. Let your child cut the slices into chunks with a butter knife. Put all the chunks in a microwave-safe bowl along with a teaspoon of water. Add a teaspoon of sugar and/or a pinch of cinnamon, if you desire. Microwave on high for three minutes or until very soft. Let cool. Your toddler can mash the cooked apple with a potato masher. He will now have a better answer to the question, "Where does applesauce come from?" besides the reply, "From the store!"

Materials: one apple, water, sugar, cinnamon, potato masher, small plastic knife

Developing Skills

- cause and effect
- fine motor coordination

Homemade Butter

Pour whipping cream into a jar with a tight-fitting lid. Do not fill it more than 2/3 full. Add a dash of salt if you wish. Take turns, with your toddler, shaking the jar. This is a good activity to do with a small group of children. Each will get several turns to shake the jar. Say a rhyme or count to twenty during each person's turn. Notice how the cream becomes thick first and then separates into a glob of butter and buttermilk as you continue shaking. Enjoy the butter on crackers.

Developing Skills

- cause and effect
- fine motor coordination

Materials: one pint heavy whipping cream, clear plastic jar

Good-Bye Song

Help your toddler anticipate the transition of leaving by singing a good-bye song. If she is resistant, don't offer many explanations about why it's time to leave. Your reasons for leaving vary, and therefore don't offer much useful information to a child. It's time to go because it's time to go. You can state what will happen next (we are going to the post office) and proceed quickly to the business of getting out the door.

Good-bye Song
(Sing to the tune of "Frère Jacques.")

Wave to Daddy, wave to Daddy.
(Substitute as necessary: Grandma, the park, etc.)
Say bye-bye, say bye-bye.
We are going to leave now.
It is time to go now.
Wave bye-bye, wave bye-bye.

Developing Skills

- understanding limits
- reinforcing routines as a pattern or sequence
- vocabulary enrichment

Play Back

Record yourself reading familiar books, reciting finger plays, and simple songs. Make an audiotape for the car. Remember to talk more slowly and distinctly than you normally would in conversation. Your toddler will enjoy following along with your voice and you can concentrate on driving.

Materials: tape player, tapes

Developing Skills

- listening
- following directions

Classical Music

Research shows some connections between stimulating the brain with classical music and later math skills. However, the child must listen to the music with focused attention. It doesn't do much good for brain development to have music playing in the background during other activities because your toddler can tune it out while focusing on the task at hand. Try playing the music while driving when she is strapped in a car seat with not much to do. It will be easier for her to focus on the music then.

Materials: classical music CDs or tapes

Developing Skills

- listening
- brain development
- exposure to music

Tether a Toy

Use plastic snap-together shower curtain rings to keep a few toys accessible while your toddler is strapped in her car seat. Link a few rings together and fasten one end around a strap near where it crosses your toddler's tummy. Keep the chain short enough that she can't wrap it around her neck. Many toys have some kind of hole or fabric loop that can be hooked on the other end of the chain. Now the toys are always within her reach, even if she drops one. When you arrive at your destination, unsnap the rings and fasten them to the stroller. No more lost toys.

Materials: linking rings or shower curtain rings, small toys

Developing Skills

- fine motor coordination
- social-emotional: independence

Go for a Drive

Every once in a while, go for a drive just to sightsee. With no other agenda, you have the freedom to stop at that construction site to watch the big trucks or watch the horses in the field. A drive can help an active toddler quiet her body and relax before nap time, too.

Materials: none

Developing Skills

- observation
- conversation

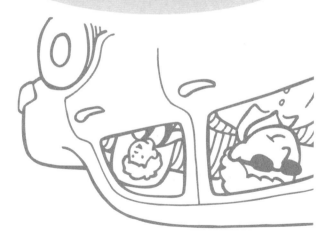

Jacket Flip

Before you can get in the car, you have to get that coat on your toddler. Build his self-help skills with this how-to-put-on-your-coat trick. Lay his coat on the floor face up. Have him stand by the neckline. A good prompt for this is, "toes by the tag." Have him line up his toes with the manufacturer's tag at the back of the neck. Now have him insert his hands into the sleeves of the coat, at the tops (not at the cuffs). He now lifts his arms, raising the coat above his head. Continue to flip the jacket over and behind his head. Voila! The coat is on right side up, ready to be zipped or buttoned.

Materials: child's coat

Developing Skills

- social-emotional: independence, self-esteem
- social-emotional: self-help skills

Shoes on the Right Feet

Help your child get his shoes on the right feet with this simple idea. Draw a dot with permanent marker or nail polish on the inside edges of the shoe soles where the big toes go. Now when the shoes are aligned properly, the dots will touch. If the shoes are reversed, the dots show on the outside edges of the shoes. Your toddler can learn to make the dots touch before slipping on his shoes.

Materials: child's shoes, permanent marker

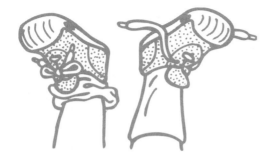

Developing Skills

- social-emotional: independence, self esteem
- social-emotional: self-help skills

Fill in the Blanks

While you are driving, recite familiar rhymes, leaving off the final word in the rhyming couplet for your toddler to finish. For example,

> **"Hickory, Dickory Dock.**
> **The mouse ran up the _____.**
> **The clock struck one**
> **And down he _____.**
> **Hickory, dickory dock."**

Developing Skills

- memory
- pre-literacy: rhyming skills

"No" Game

While you are driving, ask your child nonsense questions such as,

Can a bus fly?

Can a rock talk?

Do you have six eyes?

This gives your toddler an acceptable way to declare, "NO," one of his favorite words. Don't be surprised if some simple questions perplex your two-year-old. He has not yet developed deductive reasoning skills. Stick with concrete topics with which he has some experience.

Materials: none

Developing Skills

- receptive language
- thinking skills

Did You See That?

Look for specific vehicles while you are out and about. Say, "Let's look for motorcycles." Maybe you will spot a few. Then change to something else like mail trucks or police cars. Two-year-olds are good at learning the names of things. Differentiating among vehicles helps them sort and classify.

Materials: none

Developing Skills

- receptive language
- cognitive: matching and sorting

What's Up Doc?

Help your toddler remember, order, and classify information by asking questions about your day together. For example, "What did we eat for breakfast?" "What else do we sometimes eat for breakfast?" "What happens after bath time?" "What can we buy at the grocery store?" "Tell me something that's in the refrigerator." Toddlers have very little reasoning ability, so stick to concrete questions with concrete answers. All of her answers, right or wrong, are stimulating conversation between the two of you.

Materials: none

Developing Skills

- receptive language
- cognitive: memory

Sound Games

b,b,b,b,b, bottle.

Expose your toddler to the individual sounds in our language by breaking words down for her. Say "I hear b,b,b,b,b,b, when I say *bottle*. I hear b,b,b,b, when I say *bag*." Continue listing words that feature the sound. "*B,b,b,b box. B,b,b,b, ball.*" Also include words that feature the sound at the end. It is sometimes easier to hear a sound at the end of a word because no sound follows it. "*B,b,b,b, cab. B,b,b,b crib.*" After much repetition, your child may offer words you have said before or add one of her own.

Materials: none

Developing Skills

- receptive language
- pre-literacy: phonemic awareness

In, Out, Up, Down

Help your toddler with the concept of opposites with this game. Start with teaching her the pattern in this call-and-response format: "I'll say 'up,' you'll say 'down.' I'll say 'in,' you'll say 'out.'" After you can leave off the last word and she can fill in the blank correctly, add a new pair of opposite words, "I'll say big; you'll say _____." When your child has memorized three to five pairs, see if she can fill in the blank to a new pair without having heard that pair before.

Developing Skills

- concepts: opposites
- listening skills
- expressive skills

Variations: Add pairs as your child masters them: *wet/dry, fast/slow, boy/girl, cold/hot.*

Materials: none

I'm Thinking of an Animal

Developing Skills

- deductive reasoning
- conceptual thought
- listening skills

Describe a familiar animal with its characteristics. See if your toddler can guess what it is. Pause after each clue to give her a chance to offer an answer, for instance, "I'm thinking of an animal with a long trunk." "It has big ears." "It has tusks." "I'm thinking of an animal that has stripes." "It is black and white."

Variation: A trickier version offers clues that can apply to more than one thing. The child has to deduce the answer from more than one clue. This is difficult. "I'm thinking of something that can fly." (Kite, bird, airplane, bat, etc.) "It has wings." (Rules out kite.) "People ride in it." (Must be airplane.)

Materials: none

Compare and Contrast

Ask your toddler questions that require comparison and contrast. Again, her cognitive skills are incomplete. She does not think like adults do. Some of her answers will be funny and cute. Ask questions like, "How is a bird different from a cat? How are they the same?" "How is a motorcycle different from a car?" Remember any conversation is worthwhile. Ask her the same questions another day. Does she remember some of the answers?

Materials: none

Developing Skills

- conceptual thought
- listening skills

Food Names

While your toddler is riding in the grocery cart, hand him an item you are purchasing. He can hold and examine it while you tell him all about it. "That is a grapefruit. It's round like a ball, it is yellow, it's heavy, and we eat it for breakfast." Remove it from your toddler's hands and give him something else. "Here's a box of noodles…."

Materials: any grocery cart item

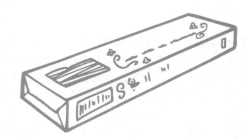

Developing Skills

- vocabulary enrichment: nouns
- concepts: attributes (color, shape)

Load 'em Up

Ever notice how your toddler often challenges his gross motor skills by carrying heavy objects? He wants to do this and he likes it. While grocery shopping, let him carry a bag of onions or some of the canned goods. You can give an item to him and instruct him to carry it back to the cart.

Materials: grocery items

Developing Skills

- gross motor coordination
- following directions

Find the Same

You are ready to check out with your groceries. Now you need to unload the entire cart. You know this will take some time and your impatient toddler had enough of shopping two aisles ago. Quickly unload as many items from the front as possible and move your toddler to where he can stand safely in the cart by your side. Ask him to hand you specific items as you name them and place them on the belt. Or, as you reach for one item, see if he can find another one just like it. Older children may be able to find an item from your description of its attributes, for instance, "It's a small, green box."

Materials: grocery items

Developing Skills

- following directions
- cognitive: attributes and same/different
- gross motor coordination

Tabloid Faces

Developing Skills

- social-emotional awareness
- vocabulary enrichment: attributes

Materials: tabloid papers

Feelings are something that will take your little one a long time to understand and be able to express appropriately. While waiting in line to check out with your groceries, make good use of those trashy tabloids by looking for happy and sad faces. At this early stage, simply draw his attention to the faces and label if they are happy or sad. Look at the features of various faces (eyebrows, mouth) and compare the faces. You can also try to imitate the differences. Finding sad, lonely or angry faces in children's books can be difficult, but some tabloids have very interesting faces that present many opportunities to talk about feelings.

20 Questions Along the Way

When your toddler is in your arms or in a shopping cart, quality face-to-face interactions are possible. Notice how many words he says in a sentence. Most toddlers respond with single words. Some toddlers are ready to build sentences with three or more words in them. Take advantage of this stage and try to compose questions that your toddler can answer such as, "Where are we going?" "What is in our shopping cart?"

Materials: none

Developing Skills

- vocabulary enrichment
- expressive language

Parking Lot Safety

Your two-year-old is growing larger everyday and sometimes it's a relief not to have to carry her everywhere. A toddler has no concept of danger, so it is really important to teach some routine habits to keep her safe. Teach her that every time she gets out of the car she needs to keep her hand on a specific spot on the car (front door handle, gas cap door, nameplate) until you take it to hold and begin walking. If you practice this every day for every trip, you will establish a habit. Toddlers learn by repetition. It will be many years before she understands the consequences of running in traffic, but she can learn that every time she gets out of the car she has a special place to touch the car and stay until you hold her hand.

Materials: none

Developing Skills

- social-emotional: waiting
- following directions
- safety rules

Navigating Stores

Sometimes your two-year-old wants to be treated like a big kid and not like a baby riding in a shopping cart or stroller. This presents a learning opportunity on how to navigate a store without touching all that tempts. So much is at eye level and very tempting for your toddler to investigate. Teach her to hold on to the cart. If she has specific things to do with her hands the temptation to touch can be lessened. Designate which bar to hold on the cart and also give her a specific place to put her free hand. If she doesn't have a pocket then show her how to tuck a thumb under her waistband on the side of her pants. Or she could carry something. This works best for brief trips.

Materials: none

Developing Skills

- understanding limits
- social-emotional: independence

Repeat Game

Ask your toddler to play the Repeat Game with you. Point to and list three items you can see and ask her to repeat them. "Truck, bus, and airplane. Can you say, truck, bus, airplane?" Build up to four words, for instance, "Stop sign, mailbox, dog, tree." Play this in the grocery store too. "Crackers, oranges, bananas, cheese." Repeating a list of four unrelated words is difficult but helps improve memory.

Materials: none

"Truck, bus, plane!"

All About Me

Sample song to the tune of "Old MacDonald:"

My name is Danni Miller

e-i-e-i-o

And I live in Ames, Iowa

e-i-e-i-o

With a 555. 8634. 555-8634

My name is Danni Miller

e-i-e-i-o

Developing Skills

- vocabulary enrichment
- social-emotional: self-awareness
- memory

Your two-year-old is ready to respond when asked, "What is your name?" Remember to practice saying both her first AND her last name. Another question she can answer is "Are you a boy or a girl?" This is a great time to make up a song about her. Children are still learning from rote so if you find the right tune she may be able to remember lots of important facts she will need to know when she gets older.

How Many?

Always carry a small box of raisins. This small box of dried fruit can buy you many minutes of activity. For example, if you are at a restaurant and your food has not yet arrived, you can draw a circle and a square on the back of a paper place mat. Pour out several raisins and give your child commands that involve early concepts of quantity.

For example, "Put *one* raisin on the circle. Put a *few* on the square. Put *more* on the circle. Take *some* off the square. Put *all* the raisins on the square." Of course, it won't spoil her appetite to eat a few, but do supervise so that she doesn't choke.

Materials: small box of raisins

Developing Skills

- fine motor coordination
- pre-math: mathematical groupings
- following directions

Simon Says

So you are in line at the bank and there is absolutely nothing with which your toddler can play. Play a simplified version of the traditional Simple Simon game using small movements. There is no need to try tricking her at this age. Just say, "Simon says" every time. This takes some careful listening and maybe even some demonstrating, but it will help pass the time. Ask your child to carry out a command involving an adverb such as, *walk slowly*, *laugh loudly*, *sit quickly*, *cough quietly*, *jump quickly*, *laugh quietly*, *cough loudly*, etc.

Materials: none

Developing Skills

- gross motor coordination
- cognitive: attributes
- vocabulary enrichment: adverbs

Find the Same Shape

Author Tana Hoban has great picture books featuring pictures of everyday objects made from simple shapes. Try *Circles, Triangles and Squares* and *Shapes, Shapes, Shapes*. After you have read one a few times at home with your toddler, you will be ready to play this game with him when out and about. Bring the book with you and turn to the circle page. Help him see what is in your immediate surroundings that is a circle. Try another shape.

Variation: Just draw the shapes on index cards and take them along to see if your toddler can find the same shapes in the environment.

Materials: a book about shapes or shapes drawn on index cards

Developing Skills
- visual discrimination
- concepts: shapes

Color of the Day

Announce to your toddler that while you're out shopping you will look for a certain color. As you go about your errands, have him look for that color. If you can, write down his observations. This is a great time to talk about light and dark shades of color. Whenever your toddler gets a little antsy, you can refocus him with, "Do you remember our color of the day? Do you see anything that color around here?" Later on, ask him what things he remembers that he saw earlier that day. Review the list together. Acknowledge his efforts regardless of how many things he actually found or recalled. "You remembered!"

Materials: none

Developing Skills

- visual discrimination
- concepts: colors
- memory

Riddles

Answering questions from clues requires deductive reasoning, a skill just dawning in older two-year-olds. Help build this ability in your toddler with riddles about the destinations of your errands. "We are going to a place where we can buy food." "We are going to the place where we buy stamps." "We need to stop somewhere to cash a check." Don't be surprised if he needs more than one clue to get the right answer.

Materials: none

Developing Skills

- cognitive: reasoning
- vocabulary enrichment

Retell the Story

Your two-year-old is gaining new words every day and he is developing the skill of organizing thoughts into words in order to tell a story. Whatever you do on your errands, verbally put it into a story he can tell when he gets home. For example, "First we went to the post office. Then we bought milk. The last thing we did was get gas for the car."

Give your two-year-old an opportunity to retell the story at home. Better yet, ask him to tell another family member when he or she gets home.

Materials: none

Developing Skills

- expressive language
- memory
- pre-literacy: sequencing

What's That Feeling Called?

Feelings are so difficult to understand. Young children do not always recognize what a feeling is, nor do they know its name. When you are near the tabloid section of the checkout lane, notice that the faces on the front covers have emotions that are obvious. Point to a face and ask your child "What do you think this person is feeling?" Giving a name to a feeling is the first step in communication. A follow-up question could be, "I wonder what could make him/her feel this way?" Your child will give you the reason that he would feel that way and that's a good thing to validate.

Materials: tabloid papers

Developing Skills

- vocabulary enrichment
- cognitive development: attributes
- social-emotional awareness

Stock Up the Diaper Bag

A well-stocked diaper bag should carry more than just the basics. In addition to a change of clothing, diapers, wipes, and such, include things to use while sitting together. Of course, you need snacks and a traveling cup. Breakfast bars or crackers make a healthy treat. Pack a few small books, little toys, a comfort item, and a little photo album. Talk about what happened in the photos. See what your toddler remembers. Change the photos occasionally to provide new topics. This is a good way to help her recognize relatives that she rarely sees. The books can be used for many activities. Have her point to things in the illustrations as you name them. Let her "read" to you. Cover a page and see what she can recall.

Materials: snacks, small photo album, books, toys, etc.

Developing Skills

- memory
- vocabulary enrichment
- following directions

Wiggling Fingers

Lift your hand way up high,
(*Raise your hand above your head.*)

Wiggle your fingers in the sky.
(*Wiggle your fingers and sway your arm.*)

Slowly bring your hand down low,
(*Lower your hand while moving it side-to-side.*)

Let it stop right here, just so.
(*Land your fingertips on your shoulder.*)

Developing Skills

- following directions
- self-awareness through body-part identification
- vocabulary enrichment

Materials: none

Face your toddler and have her copy your actions to the finger play at the left. When you complete the poem, ask your toddler, "Where did your fingers land?" If she correctly identifies the body part, respond by saying, "That's right, on your shoulder." Or if not, answer, "This is your shoulder, you are pointing to your shoulder. Can you say shoulder?"

Repeat the rhyme as long as there is interest, using a different body part each time. Include known parts like *nose, foot,* and *arm.* Add a few new ones like *neck, elbow,* and *knee.* Go back and repeat the new body parts you introduced. As your child grows, progress to *wrist, waist,* etc.

Two Little Cars

Place one car in your hand and one in your child's hand. Give commands like: "Put the car on your knee" demonstrating by placing your car on your knee. "Put the car on your chin," etc. As you say each body part, "drive" your car to the correct location on your own body. Wait for your child to follow.

Variations: As your child masters copying your actions and learns more body parts, try giving the commands and letting her try it on her own first. If she needs help, you can always show her with your car. Build up to "advanced" body parts like wrist, elbow, ankle, hip, etc.

Materials: 2 small plastic cars designed for use by children under three years old

Developing Skills

- following directions
- self-awareness through body-part identification
- vocabulary enrichment

Two Little Blackbirds

Two little blackbirds sitting on a hill.
(Hold up your index fingers in front of you.)

One named Jack, the other named Jill.
(Shake right finger on "Jack"; the left when you say "Jill.")

Fly away, Jack.
(Flutter right finger behind your back.)

Fly away, Jill.
(Flutter left finger behind back.)

Come back, Jack! Come back, Jill!
(Return each finger to the starting position.)

Developing Skills

- fine motor coordination
- focused attention
- rhyme and rhythm

There are three versions to this traditional finger play. (See pages 185 and 186 as well.) You can do all three at once or any of them separately. Sit facing your child and follow the guides for the hand motions.

Variation: Create the puppets on page 187. They are tiny and will easily fit in the diaper bag!

Materials: none; puppets optional (page 187)

Two Little Blackbirds (cont.)

Two little blackbirds sitting in the grass.
(Hold up your index fingers in front of you.)

One named Slow, one named Fast.
(Shake right finger on "slow;" the left when you say "fast.")

Fly away Slow. Fly away Fast.
(Flutter right finger behind your back.)

Come back Slow.
(Flutter left finger behind back.)

Come back Fast!
(Return each finger to the starting position.)

Developing Skills

- fine motor coordination
- focused attention
- rhyme and rhythm

See if your child recognizes this variation of "Two Little Blackbirds." The hand motions are the same as those on page 184. Change the tempo to reflect the new words (names). Draw out the word "Slow" and speed up the word "Fast."

Materials: none; puppets optional (page 187)

While Waiting

18 months and up

Two Little Blackbirds (cont.)

Two little blackbirds sitting on a cloud.
(Hold up your index fingers in front of you.)

One named Quiet, one named Loud.
(Shake right finger on "quiet;" the left when you say "loud")

Fly away Quiet. Fly away Loud.
(Flutter right finger behind your back.)

Come back Quiet.
(Flutter left finger behind back.)

Come back Loud!
(Return each finger to the starting position.)

Position yourself in front of your child. The hand motions are the same as those indicated on page 184. Note the change in wording. Change the volume of your voice to a whisper when saying the words "quiet" and raise your voice when you come to the word "loud."

Materials: none; puppets optional (page 187)

Developing Skills

- fine motor coordination
- focused attention
- rhythm and rhyme

Blackbird Puppets

If you find your toddler enjoys the "Two Little Blackbirds" rhymes, you might consider making two of these simple blackbird puppets.

Materials

2 cotton balls

2 six-inch (15 cm) circles of black fabric

Glitter glue or google eyes

6" (15 cm) black yarn

small orange diamond (Fold to form a beak.)

Assembly: Place a cotton ball in the center of the black piece of fabric. Enclose the cotton ball and tie the black string around the bunched fabric. Decorate with glitter glue or google eyes and an orange beak. Repeat the process for the second blackbird puppet.

Place one puppet on each index finger when presenting the rhyme.

The Truck Song

Oh, the backhoe digs a big hole
Bump, bump, bump.

(*Bounce toddler in your lap on "bump."*)

**The backhoe digs a big hole
Bump, bump, bump.
The backhoe digs a big hole.
The backhoe digs a big hole.
The backhoe digs a big hole
Bump, bump, bump.**

Additional verses:

**The dump truck pours the dirt out
Tip, tip, tip.**

(*Tip the toddler back.*)

**The Bobcat backs up slowly,
Beep, beep, beep.**

(*Gently press the toddler's nose on "beep."*)

Lots of toddlers love construction vehicles and they still love bouncy lap games, too. Sing this to the tune of "She'll be Comin' 'Round the Mountain When She Comes."

Variation: Change the song to animals:

The camel walks along bump, bump, bump.

The horse rears up and back, tip, tip, tip.

The driver beeps his horn beep, beep, beep.

Developing Skills

- vocabulary enrichment
- pre-literacy: rhyme and rhythm

Lipstick Relay

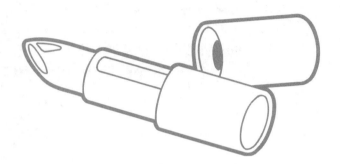

Always carry a tube of lipstick or lip balm. Here are simple games to play while waiting for doctor appointments. A small end table within the office makes a great surface across which to roll the tube. Clear off the table and station yourself on one side; have your toddler stationed on the opposite side. Take turns rolling the tube between the two of you. It is a great way to begin teaching the skills of waiting and turn-taking.

Variations: Sit on the floor opposite each other and practice rolling the tube back and forth. With sibling(s), sit in a circle and pass from one person to the next. Hide the lipstick while your toddler covers her eyes. Depending on her skill level, you may need to leave a portion of it visible.

Materials: a lipstick or lip balm tube

Developing Skills

- fine motor coordination
- social-emotional: taking turns
- problem solving

I Spy

Young toddlers are just beginning to understand symbolic representation. Your toddler demonstrates this when she places a block (as a substitute for food) in a toy pan and serves it to you. While you are waiting, open up your purse, wallet, organizer, or pocket and have your toddler observe all the items inside. Give clues about those objects and see if she can guess what you are thinking of. "I see some things that make a jingling sound. I use them to start the car. I use them to unlock the doors." At this early stage the game is best played with a limited amount of things from which to choose.

Variations: describe objects in the waiting room. Describe items from a page in a magazine.

Materials: none

Developing Skills

- visual discrimination: size and shape
- cognitive: object identification by function

Here Is a Beehive

Although accurate counting skills can be two years away, hearing the numbers recited in order exposes your child to the skill. At this age, counting finger plays are more about fine motor manipulation of the fingers and the pre-literacy skills of rhyme, rhythm, and repetition, but they will help set a foundation for future math skills, as well. Teach this rhyme with one fist extended in front of you.

Developing Skills

- pre-math: exposure to counting
- pre-literacy: rhyme and rhythm
- fine motor coordination

Here is a Beehive

Here is a beehive.
(Tuck your thumb inside your fist.)

Where are all the bees?
Hidden away where nobody sees.
(Hide your fist behind your back.)

Soon they come flying out of the hive.
(Return your fist to the front.)

One, two, three, four, five!
(Pop each finger up.)

Buzz, buzz, buzz!
(Wiggle your fingers all around.)

I Wiggle My Fingers

With a little luck you will be able to use this poem to focus a wiggly child while waiting in line, or in a restaurant. Use the opportunity to acknowledge desirable behavior with positive statements such as, "Look how quietly you are sitting; you are waiting so patiently."

I Wiggle My Fingers

I wiggle my fingers. I wiggle my nose.

(Wiggle fingers, wiggle nose.)

I wiggle my shoulders. I wiggle my toes.

(Wiggle shoulders, wiggle toes.)

'Til no more wiggles are left in me,

(Hold upturned palms in front of you.)

And I sit still and quietly.

(Place folded hands in your lap.)

Developing Skills

- pre-literacy: rhyme and rhythm
- fine motor coordination
- social-emotional: self-control

Here Is a Bunny

Here Is a Bunny

Here is a bunny with ears so funny.

(Hold up one hand with two fingers, slightly curved, for ears.)

Here is his hole in the ground.

(Use the other hand to form a hole with a loosely closed fist.)

When a noise he hears,

He perks up his ears.

(Say, "Boo!" and extend and stiffen your two finger-ears.)

And jumps in his hole in the ground!

(Insert finger-ears into the other hand's hole.)

Developing Skills

- pre-literacy: rhyme and rhythm
- fine motor coordination

One Elephant Went Out to Play

One Elephant Went Out to Play

One elephant went out to play

(Hold up one finger.)

On a spider's web one day.

(Crawl your fingers like an itsy bitsy spider.)

He had such enormous fun,

(Circle your arms wide overhead and down to your sides.)

He called for another elephant to come,

"Hey, elephant!"

(Cup hands by mouth and shout.)

Here he comes!

(Slap knees in slow, lumbering footsteps.)

Additional verses: Repeat with two elephants.
Continue with three. After the last line, "Here he
comes," say, "Oh no, the web broke!"

Developing Skills

- pre-literacy: rhyme and rhythm
- memory
- fine motor coordination

Color/Shape Match Game

Point out to your toddler an object in the room that is a certain color or shape and then find other objects in the room that match. Say, "Find one like this." Sometimes it is easier to find matching items in a picture in a magazine, so start with that if your toddler is not yet ready to find matching items around the room. Also, keep in mind that children can often discriminate and match colors or shapes before they can correctly name them.

Materials: none

Developing Skills

- concepts: color and shape
- matching
- pre-literacy: visual discrimination

Beginning Writing

The diaper bag should always be supplied with a notepad of unlined paper and a pencil. They can be used for a number of activities and games. Here is a copycat game. Draw a line horizontally across the paper. Ask your two-year-old to draw one like it. Now draw a vertical line and ask him to make one like that. Can he copy a circle? He may be ready to copy all that you draw. The importance of this game is to praise any attempt. Controlling the pencil to make specific lines is harder than scribbling. Practicing strokes that differ in direction is an excellent pre-writing activity.

Variation: For older children, make some simple letters to copy: C, X, L, V, T.

Materials: unlined paper and pencil

Developing Skills

- fine motor coordination
- pre-literacy: visual tracking
- pre-writing: copying shapes

Forbidden Fruit

Now is a perfect time to let your toddler explore those items of purse and pocket that are normally off limits. He can safely and quietly examine a make-up mirror or rubber band while sitting in your lap. Let him pull your credit cards out of the plastic pockets and reinsert them for some fine motor work. He will enjoy pushing the buttons on a calculator. Naming the objects and describing their functions introduces new words.

Materials: objects from your purse

Developing Skills

- curiosity and discovery
- fine motor coordination
- vocabulary enrichment

I Caught a Fish Alive

Developing Skills

- pre-math: exposure to counting
- memory
- fine motor coordination

One, two, three, four, five,
(Extend one finger at a time as you count.)

Once I caught a fish alive!
(Clap hands together.)

Six, seven, eight, nine, ten,
(Extend the fingers of the other hand.)

Then I let it go again.
(Pantomime a dropping motion.)

Why did you let it go?
(Hold palms up in questioning gesture.)

Because it bit my finger so!
(Make this declaration with hands on hips.)

Which finger did it bite?
(Hold palms up in questioning gesture.)

The little finger on the right!
(Hold up and wiggle your pinky.)

I Had a Little Turtle

Developing Skills

- pre-literacy: rhyme and rhythm
- memory
- fine motor coordination

I Had a Little Turtle

I had a little turtle; he lived inside a box.
(Form a turtle with your hands.)

He swam into the water;
He climbed upon the rocks.
(Make paddling motions with hands, then walk fingers along leg.)

He snapped at a mosquito;
He snapped at a flea;
(Snap to the left with index finger and thumb; snap to the right.)

He snapped at a minnow;
And he snapped at me.
(Snap to the left; snap toward self.)

He caught the mosquito; he caught the flea,
(Clap hands together to the left; clap to the right.)

He caught the minnow; but he didn't catch me!
(Clap to the left, point to self and shake head, "No.")

Ten Little Fingers

I have ten little fingers,
And they all belong to me.
(Hold up extended fingers, then hug self.)

I can make them do things.
Would you like to see?

I can shut them up tight,
(Make fists.)

Or open them up wide.
(Spread open fingers.)

Developing Skills

- pre-literacy: rhyme and rhythm
- memory
- fine motor coordination

I can put them all together,
(Interlace your fingers.)

Or, I can make them hide.
(Hide your fingers behind your back.)

I can make them jump high,
(Reach above your head.)

I can make them jump low.
(Reach downward.)

I can roll them all around,
And hold them just so.
(Roll your hands over each other then place your hands in your lap.)

Variation: After your child knows this poem well, see if she can remember all the motions while you just say the words.

Five Little Ducks

Five little ducks went out to play,

(Hold up five fingers.)

Over the hill and far away,

(Raise hand in an arc then hide it behind your back.)

**The mother duck called,
"Quack, quack, quack!"**

(Make a duck beak with your other hand, all fingers together opposite your thumb.)

Four little ducks came waddling back.

(Bring four fingers out from behind your back.)

Developing Skills

- pre-literacy: rhyme and rhythm
- pre-math: counting
- fine motor coordination

Additional verses: Continue counting down until, "No little ducks came waddling back."

Last verse:

Sad mother duck went out one day,

(Make a sad face.)

Over the hill and far away,

(Raise the duck beak hand in an arc then hide it behind your back.)

**The mother duck called,
"Quack, quack, quack!"**

(Shout with your duck beak hand in front of you.)

And five little ducks came waddling back!

(Have five fingers return from behind your back.)

Letter Match Game

This game involves matching letters on a page. For a child of this age to be successful at this game, you need to isolate the letter you are trying to match and define the area where to look. Find an ad in a magazine that has duplicate letters. Using two small pieces of paper, surround a single letter. Keep that letter isolated. Place the edge of another piece of paper below, and one above, the line of text you want your child to search through to find the match. Allow her to slide her finger across the line, searching for the matching letter. This pre-reading skill promotes the pattern of beginning on the left side and going across the page to the right side.

Materials: magazine, plain paper strips

Developing Skills

- pre-literacy: visual discrimination
- identifying letters
- pre-literacy: visual tracking

Find Something Longer

Keep a small measuring tape in your purse, pocket, or diaper bag. It is a necessity for those long waits in the doctor's office.

Two-year-olds love the opportunity to play with *real* tools. Your child can measure everything as you read the numbers. This is also a way to introduce the concept of comparing sizes. Pull the tape out to a certain length. Then have your toddler find things that are longer than the measurement on the tape.

Variation: Find things that are smaller, or the same size.

Materials: measuring tape

Developing Skills

- concepts: size comparisons
- vocabulary enrichment: comparative and superlative words
- problem solving

Fingertip Touch

Touch your thumb to each of your fingertips in turn and encourage your child to imitate. You could count as each fingertip is touched. At first, she will make errors and perform the task slowly, but with practice she should be able to touch her thumb to each finger. This may be one of the places where you can see your child start to demonstrate a hand preference.

Materials: none

Developing Skills

- fine motor development
- eye-hand coordination

Paint the Garage

Give your toddler a bucket of water and a wide paintbrush. Let him paint the garage, the fence, the sidewalk, etc. The wet spots look darker, so he can tell where he's already painted.

Variation: Let your toddler step in water and make footprints on the sidewalk. It's fun to watch them evaporate on a hot day.

Materials: large paint brush, bucket of water

Developing Skills

- gross motor coordination
- pretend play

The Backyard or Park

18 months and up

What Do You Hear?

A good game to play while walking along the street with your toddler is "What Do You Hear?" When you're outside, you hear many animal sounds. See if your toddler can identify and imitate those sounds. How about car and truck sounds? Can he copy any of those?

Materials: none

Developing Skills

- vocabulary enrichment
- pre-literacy: auditory discrimination

Visual Scavenger Hunt

Help your toddler learn to visually scan an area. Ask him to point to the items you name. Choose things from a wide area of vision so that he'll need to look up, down, and to both sides. You might say, for instance, "I see a squirrel. Where is it?" "I see a puddle, mailbox, cloud, stop sign, etc."

Variation: Make a list to check off. When you return home, ask him how many things he remembers. Give him clues.

Materials: none

Developing Skills

- vocabulary enrichment: nouns
- pre-literacy: visual scanning
- memory

The Backyard or Park   *18 months and up*

Getting There

Physically walking to the park is sometimes difficult because your toddler is entering a very independent stage. He wants to do everything for himself. Have him push the stroller or pull the wagon to the park himself. Place a piece of colored tape where you want him to hold on to the stroller. He won't be so frustrated with his inability to reach the handles and it will help him to focus on the task. He will likely appreciate a ride home after he has tired himself out.

Materials: stroller, colored tape

Developing Skills

- eye-hand coordination
- gross motor skills
- social-emotional: independence

Riding Pedal Toys

Developing Skills

- bilateral coordination
- understanding limits
- vocabulary enrichment (start, stop, go, wait)

Let your toddler ride his tricycle to the corner. Keep him safe with the following ideas. Some wheel toys are noisy and he may not be able to hear you say stop. For children under three, it is best to put a leash around the seat of the trike. This keeps you in control of the speed and you can stop him. Make a big **X**, or draw a stop sign, with chalk on the sidewalk wherever you want him to stop. Toddlers have no rules in their heads that help them know the boundaries of the sidewalk and street. Safety will have to be taught by calling his attention to the **X**s. Even after you have defined the boundaries, you will need to enforce them. *Never* expect a toddler to remember. *Always* stay close by to control the movement of the wheel toy.

Materials: leash or rope, chalk, tricycle

No Equipment Needed

Sometimes a park can be unsafe for young toddlers. Perhaps the equipment has large spaces that he could fall through. There may be many older children playing nearby who won't be watching out for your little one. When the play area is not suitable, move away from the action and practice some gross motor skills. Can your toddler copy you as you cross your feet and stand for a few minutes? Can he bend at his waist, touch the ground, and return to standing without losing his balance? While holding your hand, can he balance on the left foot and then the right foot? How long can he stay in a squatting position? Can your toddler walk on tiptoe for a short distance? Count how long he maintains a position to gauge his progress.

Materials: none

Developing Skills

- balance
- cross-lateral coordination

Old Play Dough Fossils

When your play dough is getting too stiff to work with easily, use it for one more project. Take it outside and have your toddler experiment with textures and impressions. Flatten the dough into several thick "pancakes." Show him how to press one lightly into the bark of a tree. Peel it off and observe the impression left. Let him make an impression of concrete or grass, pinecones, rocks, and leaves. Talk about the textures. Name the nature objects. These can be painted after they are completely dry.

Developing Skills

- fine motor coordination
- sensory exploration of texture
- vocabulary enrichment

Variation: See if your toddler can remember which pattern was made by which object.

Materials: old play dough

The Backyard or Park

18 months and up

Wash the Car

Your toddler will appreciate having a scrub brush and pail of his own. A fingernail brush is the right size for him. Give him a bucket of soapy water and a job to do. He can scrub the wheels while you wash the rest of the car. It's fun to watch more bubbles appear as you scrub. Toddlers like repetition. He may want to clean the tires even when the rest of the car doesn't need a wash. He can also wash his riding toys.

Materials: child-size scrub brush, bucket of water

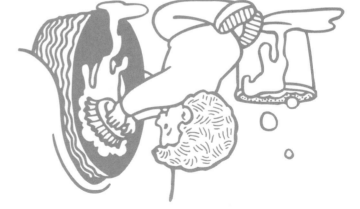

Developing Skills

- fine motor coordination
- sensory exploration of texture
- vocabulary enrichment: nouns

Boundaries

Developing Skills

- understanding limits

Toddlers are concrete thinkers. They do best when instructions and limits are made as clear as possible. Help her learn what, "Stay in the yard" and "Don't go by the street," mean with these ideas. Use chalk to draw a line across the driveway about ten feet from the road. That is as far as she can walk or ride her tricycle. Practice this with a stop-and-go game so she learns not to cross the line. If you don't have a fenced backyard, tie ribbons in the shrubbery and around the tree trunks to create a visual reminder of the boundary. Always supervise her and if she strays beyond the boundaries, she loses her opportunity to play outside. Play inside for awhile and then come outside and try again. Through consistent reinforcement, she'll come to understand.

Materials: chalk, ribbon

The Backyard or Park

24 months and up

Ant Hill

Place a few cracker crumbs by an anthill. Check back later with your toddler to see if the ants have discovered your gift. Toddlers like to notice and observe little details, and the ants are fascinating. Watch them carry big pieces of cracker. See them march in a line. Where are they going?

Materials: a cracker

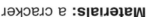

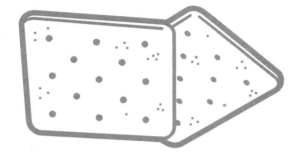

Developing Skills

- observing nature
- conversation

Show Me the Action

It is difficult for toddlers to speak with action words. Walks to the park present lots of opportunities to observe and talk about actions. See if you can turn the activities around you into questions to which your toddler can *point out* the answer, such as, "Can you show me the boy who's running?" or "Who is climbing the ladder?" Live examples of actions are the best way to learn the verbs that go with them.

Materials: none

Developing Skills

- vocabulary enrichment: verbs
- observation

Jumping Time

Your two-year-old is beginning to have more control over her body. She may be able to jump. Here are some of the gross motor activities that you can begin to encourage. Have her maintain her balance while jumping from a 6" (15 cm) high surface with both feet together. After success with this, try eight to ten inches. Demonstrate a forward jump. Encourage her to jump forward as far as possible. Four to fourteen inches is a normal range. Demonstrate walking backwards and then ask her to walk backwards. Demonstrate hopping on one foot. Hold her hand and see if she can copy you.

Variation: See if your child can quickly change directions while running.

Materials: none

Developing Skills

- gross motor skills
- balance

Sticks and Stones

Toddlers love to gather natural objects that they find outside. Have your toddler sort the objects into piles. Stones can go in one pile, and sticks in another. Next, show her how to sort the stones by an attribute, maybe size or color. Sort the sticks by long and short. Lay out a pattern for her to copy, such as, stick, stone, stick, stone. Try giving directions that use spatial concepts, for instance, "Put the stone under the leaf," "Put a stick next to my foot," "Hold a stone behind your back."

Materials: found objects

Developing Skills

- concepts: matching and sorting
- pre-math: recognizing patterns
- concepts: spatial/temporal relationships

Chalk Line Games

Draw a straight line at least six feet long on the driveway, sidewalk, or playground asphalt. Show your toddler how to walk with both feet along the line. Try walking on a squiggly line. How about a zigzagging line? Have her try walking on tiptoe, or in "brick step" with heel touching toe. Later try the more complicated cross-lateral step. This step involves stepping crisscross over the line without touching it.

Variation: Try the same activities walking on a 2" x 4" (5 cm x 10 cm) board lying on the ground.

Materials: chalk

Developing Skills

- balance
- cross-lateral coordination

Leaves in the Air

Let your toddler spin and run around with fall leaves as her inspiration with this song. Remind her to use her arms, too.

Leaves in the Air

(Sing to the tune of "Row, Row, Row Your Boat.")

Leaves, leaves in the air,
Swirling orange and brown.
(Run and twirl freely.)

Leaves, leaves from the trees,
Falling to the ground.
(Drop to the ground.)

Developing Skills

- balance
- gross motor coordination

Snowflakes Falling

Sometimes there isn't as much to do outside in the winter. This song gives direction to your toddler's movements.

Snowflakes Falling

(Sing to the tune of "Mary Had a Little Lamb.")

Snowflakes falling from the clouds,
From the clouds, from the clouds.
(Let child freely spin or run.)

Snowflakes falling all around,
Landing on the fence.
(The child runs to that place.)
Repeat the song, changing the last word (porch, car, sandbox).

Developing Skills

- balance
- gross motor coordination
- following directions

The Big Swing

Your young child is becoming more and more confident of his motor skills. He is ready to explore swings and learn how to pump. He will need to be reminded about how to stay safe on a standard swing by holding on at all times. He needs to let you know verbally when he wants to get off, rather than just letting go. Swinging gives opportunities to increase vocabulary by understanding spatial-temporal relationships: *up*, *down*, *underneath*, *on top of*, *backward* and *forward*, *above*, and *below*.

Developing Skills

- gross motor coordination
- vocabulary enrichment
- spatial concepts

Materials: a swing

More Ways to Move

Once your toddler has mastered running, there are other motor patterns he can practice. Show him how to step sideways in one direction, always leading with the same foot. As you go faster this becomes a slide. Try leading with the opposite foot and go the other way. Galloping is similar, except the motion is forward. Lead with the same foot. Have him try it with the other foot. Remember, when limbs on each side of the body are doing different things, the right and left brain hemispheres must communicate in a more sophisticated way.

Materials: none

Developing Skills

- gross motor coordination
- bilateral coordination

Balls, Balls, Balls

Bring a few toys from home to increase the time you stay at the park. Use an old pillowcase as a ball sack. Include a large soft rubber ball, a smaller tennis size ball, and one that is really big. Have your toddler roll on top of the biggest ball. Hold his feet and roll him around while he tries to balance on his tummy. The medium size ball is a good one for catching. The smallest ball is for practice throwing overhand. See if he can hit a large target (a fence or tree).

Materials: balls of various sizes

Developing Skills

- fine motor coordination
- eye-hand coordination
- gross motor coordination

Four Things at Once

As a parent, you are familiar with the very complex skill of multi-tasking. Increase your toddler's skills with a game of multi-tasking. Find a safe place where he can walk away from you and return to you. Give him two things to do in addition to walking away and returning to you. See if he remembers all four things. This is a very difficult task. You should start by having him follow a one-step direction, then a two-step, and then a three-step direction. Finally, you will be ready for four steps. Try this, "Walk to the tree. Pick up the ball. Put it by the house and then come back to the wagon."

Materials: none

Developing Skills

- following directions
- pre-literacy: sequencing
- memory

Shape Game

This game combines learning shapes with gross motor activity. Two-year-olds like to be on the move. Bring a roll of masking tape outside. With the tape, make the outline of a circle on the side of the garage, your apartment, or a wall at the park. Tape a square at least a few feet away. Tell your toddler to run to one of the shapes. Have him return to you before he is sent to another shape.

Variation: Include other shapes like a triangle, diamond, and star.

Materials: masking tape

Developing Skills

- visual discrimination
- auditory memory
- concepts: shapes

Hop, Clap, Hop

Another way to reinforce patterns is with movement. Create a motion pattern for your toddler to follow. Demonstrate the motions for him and then do it with him until he can follow a verbal direction alone.

Try ABAB patterns first such as, stomp, clap, stomp, clap. Add a C to make ABCABC patterns: clap, stomp, turn around, clap, stomp, turn around.

Variations: These get very challenging very quickly: ABBABB, AABBAABB, ABACABAC. Can your toddler make a new pattern?

Materials: none

Developing Skills

- pre-math: recognizing patterns
- gross motor coordination
- following directions

Who's First?

At the park there will likely be other children playing. Their presence will provide good opportunities to teach some spatial-temporal relationships you just can't teach at home. While your toddler is waiting in line for a turn on the slide, try using the words *first*, *next*, *last*, *before*, and *after*. For example, "The girl with the red shirt is *first*, the boy is *next*, and you are *after* him." You can also practice manners like teaching him to keep his hands to himself, learning how to greet someone, waiting, and respecting personal space. "We will stand here so everyone has enough room to feel comfortable."

Materials: none

Developing Skills

- vocabulary enrichment
- spatial concepts
- social-emotional: taking turns, waiting

Homemade Bird Feeders

With your toddler, tie a string to one end of a pinecone. Spread peanut butter or vegetable shortening on the pinecone or a 2" x 6" piece of cardboard (5 cm x 15 cm). Next, have your toddler help you gently press the pinecone or cardboard in a tray of birdseed. Once it is well coated, hang it by the string loop on a tree branch or from the rafters. The strip of cardboard can be nailed directly to the trunk, if you prefer.

Materials: large pinecones, string, cardboard, peanut butter or vegetable shortening, mixed birdseed

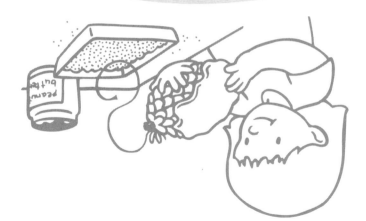

Developing Skills
- vocabulary enrichment
- fine motor coordination
- observing nature

Glossary of Developmental Skills

Attributes: characteristics or qualities of objects or abstract concepts. For example, size words include: *big*, *huge*, *large*, *tiny*, and *small*. Shape words include: *long*, *thin*, *wide*, *round*, and *flat*. Texture words: *rough*, *bumpy*, *smooth*, and *slippery*.

Auditory discrimination: the ability to tell sounds apart. Recognizing a voice from others, rhyming words, or distinguishing letter sounds requires auditory discrimination.

Bilateral coordination: the ability to coordinate the movements of both sides of the body to produce smooth actions like running or pedaling a tricycle.

Cause and effect: recognizing the consequences of a given action. Understanding that the same action results in the same effect. Also, seeing cause and effect in processes like turning lumber into wood, or cream into butter.

Cross-lateral movement: the ability to move one's hand or foot over to the opposite side, crossing the midline of the body.

Glossary of Developmental Skills (cont.)

Eye-hand/eye-foot coordination: coordinating the movement of one's hand or foot with the information one receives visually, like the distance and speed of a moving object. Catching and throwing require eye-hand coordination.

Emotional awareness: the ability to recognize feelings and distinguish one feeling from another.

Expressive language: the extent to which one can communicate one's thoughts to others. This communication can be non-verbal (gestures, body language, crying), but toddlers increase their spoken vocabularies to include verbs and attributes that help them develop conceptual thought.

Fine motor coordination: controlling the muscles of the wrist, hand, and fingers in a purposeful way. Fine motor skills are required to open doors, unscrew lids, zip and button, and hold a pencil.

Gross motor coordination: controlling the large muscles of the body in purposeful movements like walking, running, hopping, kicking, balancing, throwing, catching, and jumping.

Motor patterns: coordinated repetitive movements like walking, running, galloping, skipping, and skating.

Glossary of Developmental Skills (cont.)

Phonemic awareness: the ability to tell letter sounds apart and recognize the individual sounds that make up words.

Pre-literacy skills: any activity that promotes understanding language and its written form, such as, building vocabulary, looking at books, listening to stories, learning rhymes, and rhythms of speech.

Purposeful movement: guiding gross or fine motor movements to achieve a specific purpose.

Receptive language: when being spoken to, the extent to which one can understand voice intonation, inflection, and words spoken.

Reinforcing routines: repeating a sequence of events or tasks to promote recall, memory, sequencing, patterning, anticipation, and security.

Sensory discrimination: the ability to tell sensory input apart, such as textures, sounds, and smells.

Sensory motor play: experiences that integrate movement and tactile (touch) experiences such as, playing in sand, swimming, playing with play dough.

Spatial/temporal relationships: understanding concepts of space and time: *under*, *over*, *through*, *beside*, *behind*, *next*, *last*, *tomorrow*, *later*, *now*.

Glossary of Developmental Skills (cont.)

Symbolic representation: understanding that something "stands for" something else. A block can represent a vehicle or food during pretend play. Letters represent the sounds of our spoken language; numerals represent quantity.

Visual discrimination: the ability to tell things apart by how they look in finer and finer detail. This skill is needed to tell similar letters apart.

Visual memory: the ability to form a mental image of something seen. Forming a picture in the mind's eye helps with spatial concepts.

Visual tracking: the ability to follow the movement of an object with one's eyes. This skill is needed for following and catching a ball being thrown or to follow a line of text in a book.

Vocabulary enrichment: building the number of known words through repetition and exposure. Learning the words for math concepts, spatial/temporal relationships, and attributes help toddlers build the cognitive ability for abstract thought.

Understanding limits: knowing that some choices are not available. This is the foundation for rules and for future self-control.

Developmental Milestones

Children's growth and development doesn't follow a steady, smooth, upward path. It is more common to see your child grow quickly in some areas, stall in another, and backslide a little in other areas. Growth spurts and plateaus are the rule, not the exception. It is better to look for continuous progress over time rather than link a specific skill to a specific timetable. It is also hard to isolate developmental skills. A child's sensory, motor, cognitive, and language development are intertwined and feed off each other. Improving cognitive skills helps build language ability; increasing language skills helps build cognitive function. Children learn most things by absorbing them indirectly from contact with their environment. Your interaction and support provide the secure emotional foundation from which a child draws energy to explore and experiment. Learning is embedded in daily life.

Look for growing skills demonstrated in everyday situations. The following are examples of activities or situations where skills can be revealed. The skills are grouped loosely in "early" or "late" developing categories, and are listed in no particular order within groupings.

Developmental Milestones (cont.)

Fine Motor

Early Skills: imitates a crayon stroke, strings large beads, scoops with a spoon or shovel, throws a small ball, pounds and squeezes clay, twists at wrist to invert a container, scribbles.

Later Skills: unscrews a jar lid, aligns blocks horizontally, snips with scissors, places tiny objects in small containers, imitates a vertical line, circle, and horizontal line, pounds pegs, touches fingertips to thumb, stacks several blocks in a tower.

Gross Motor

Early Skills: carries heavy objects while walking, walks backward, stands on one foot with support, jumps from a single step.

Later Skills: jumps forward, avoids obstacles while running, walks up stairs with alternating feet, pedals a tricycle, catches a large ball with arms and body, hops on one foot.

Developmental Milestones (cont.)

Language

Early Skills: points to several common objects when asked, names three body parts, follows one-step directions, understands simple concepts like "in" and "under," has 15-20 word vocabulary, uses inflection and intonation, puts two words together.

Later Skills: names many common objects, names eight body parts, uses past tense, pronouns, and prepositions, uses size and quantity words, builds sentences of five words or more, answers "who," "what," and "where" questions.

Cognitive

Early Skills: explores environment, matches objects, matches sound to animal, identifies personal property, remembers where objects belong, sorts by one attribute like color, begins symbolic play.

Later Skills: finds details in pictures, engages in simple make-believe activities, acting out familiar actions, categorizes objects (foods, vehicles, clothing), understands *two*, points to colors when named, understands simple spatial concepts like *front*, *back*, *upside down*, *open* and *closed*, identifies objects by touch, sequences three-step processes, names a missing object when one of three is removed.

Developmental Milestones (cont.)

Independence/Self-Help Skills

Early Skills: drinks from open cup, feeds self using fingers and utensils, attempts dressing/undressing, can do simple snaps or zippers, indicates needs and desires by pointing or words.

Later Skills: feeds self with spoon and fork, pours liquid into a glass, washes hands and face with assistance, puts on T-shirt, puts on a coat, shows interest in potty training.

Social-Emotional

Early Skills: says "no" and "mine," is possessive of toys, uses greetings when reminded, may have separation issues, expresses affection physically, has greater range of emotions, tantrums easily, puts toys away with assistance, stays on task for at least three to five minutes.

Later Skills: plays independently, wants to help with household tasks, can wait a little bit, identifies boys and girls, begins to understand simple rules, takes turns with some prompting, understands some feelings, enjoys the company of another child, needs help to solve conflicts.

Suggested Activities by Skill

Fine Motor Skills

General coordination: Egg Beater Bubbles 19, Simple Puzzles 87, Stringing Beads 91, Nuts and Bolts 99, Simple Art Activities 110-132

Grasp/release: Sponge Squeeze 85, Tongs Transfer 94, Eye Droppers 102, Scissors Snip 121

Eye-hand coordination: Balls and Nets 29, Bat the Beach Ball 58, Magnetic Fishing 59, Hammer and Nails 68, Stamping 119, Copy with Markers 124, Balls, Balls, Balls 223

Pre-writing: Writing on the Wall 26, Clean Windows 41, Write and Squish 103, Copy with Markers 124, Beginning Writing 196, Letter Match Game 202

Gross Motor Skills

General coordination: Laundry Learning 34, Garden Help 46, Grocery Bag Blocks 55, Stop and Go Music 56, Bean Bag Games 60, 71, 72, 73

Balance: Bean Bag Game 3 72, Walk the Line 74, No Equipment Needed 210, Jumping Time 216, Leaves in the Air 219

Bilateral/cross lateral coordination: Advanced Head, Shoulders, Knees, and Toes 79, Riding Pedal Toys 209, No Equipment Needed 210, Chalk Line Games 218, More Ways to Move 222

Suggested Activities by Skill (cont.)

Sensory Skills: The Sensory Table Box 80, 93, What Does it Feel Like? 98, Gloop 100, Glurch 101, Matching by Sound 106, Matching by Taste 107, Finger Paint Pudding 112, Gingerbread Boy 125

Language Skills

Receptive Skills: Empty the Dishwasher 38, Shake and Stop 65, Go Fetch 88, Food Names 165, Simon Says 175, Forbidden Fruit 197, Show Me the Action 215

Expressive Skills: Water Words 27, More Laundry Learning 44, Sensory Table Math 82, Play Dough Ideas 84, In, Out, Up, Down 162, Twenty Questions Along the Way 169

Pre-literacy Skills

General Skills: Books in Bed 18, Daily Reading 24, Bedtime: Mommy Is Reading 32, Story Book Extensions 61–62, Tongs Transfer 94, Puppet Theatre 108, Retell the Story 179

Auditory Skills, Rhyme and Rhythm: Matching by Sound 106, Fill in the Blanks 157, Sound Games 161, Finger Plays 184-188, 191-194, 198-201, What Do you Hear? 206

Matching, Sequencing, Patterning: See Cognitive Skills

Suggested Activities by Skill (cont.)

Cognitive Skills

Cause and Effect: Drinking from a Cup 22, Dusting 40, Garden Help 46, Toddler Crayons 113, Golf Ball Painting 123, Homemade Apple Sauce 148, Homemade Butter 149

Memory: Go Fetch 88, Memory Recall 105, What's Up, Doc? 160, All About Me 173, Retell the Story 179, Visual Scavenger Hunt 207

Color: Magnetic Fishing 59, Color Hunt 70, Matching 96, Sorting 97, Color Squish 116, Color of the Day 177, Color/Shape Match Game 195

Shape: Clean Windows 41, Matching 96, Sorting 97, Find the Same Shape 176, Color/Shape Match Game 195, Shape Game 225

Pre-math: Balls and Nets 29, Setting the Table 51, Beanbag Game 1 60, Sensory Table Math 82, Snack Mix 135, Banana Rounds 144, How Many? 174, Here Is a Beehive 191

Matching/Sorting: Empty the Dishwasher 38, Organize the Toys 39, More Laundry Learning 44, Clean Up Time 45, Color Hunt 70, Sorting 97, Nuts and Bolts 99, Did You See That? 159, Sticks and Stones 217

Sequencing: Diaper Distractions 12, Glue Stick 115, Painting with Glue 126, Put it All Together 129, Sailboats 143, Who's First? 227

Patterning: Storybook Extensions 61-62, Patterning 109, Stamping 119, Fruit Kabobs 147, Sticks and Stones 217, Hop, Clap, Hop 226

Reasoning: Snack in a Jar 141, I'm Thinking of an Animal 163, Compare and Contrast 164, Riddles 178

Suggested Activities by Skill (cont.)

Social/Emotional Skills

Emotional Awareness: Happy and You Know It 67, Mirror, Mirror on the Wall 89, Tabloid Faces 168, What's That Feeling Called? 180

Self-Control: Stop-and-Go Music 56, Shake and Stop 65, Lipstick Relay 189, I Wiggle My Fingers 192, Who's First? 227

Understanding Limits: Diaper Distractions 12, Nap Choices 17, Good-Bye Song 150, Parking Lot Safety 170, Navigating Stores 171, Riding Pedal Toys 209, Boundaries 213

Independence/Self-help Skills: Drinking From a Cup 22, Nap Sacks 30, Mealtime Clean-Up 36, Organize the Toys 39, Clean Sweep 48, Pour it On 49, Refrigerator Snacks 50, Pitcher to Pitcher 95, Jacket Flip 155, Shoes on the Right Feet 156

Self Esteem: Family Placemats 23, Bedtime Foot Massage 25, Why Household Chores? 33, Mealtime Clean-Up 36, Clean Sweep 48, Pour it On 49